"Karen Ehman's books are always delightfully full—helpful, useful, playful, meaningful. Every chapter is brimming with personal experiences, practical tips, and deliciously simple recipes. *Reach Out, Gather In* is an ideal source of encouragement for those of us who might not have the spiritual gift of hospitality but really want to make others welcome. Friends, this is the book we've been waiting for."

Liz Curtis Higgs, bestselling author of *The Girl's Still Got It*

"Karen is masterful at inspiring us to open our homes for heartfelt hospitality as well as beautifully showing us how to do this simply and with a generous heart. This book is soul-filling and heartwarming."

Sally Clarkson, host of the *At Home With Sally* podcast,
author of *Desperate*, *Own Your Life*, and *Awaking Wonder*

"As someone who's intimidated by hospitality, I need a guide, someone inspirational as well as practical. Karen Ehman will give you the confidence and courage you need to open your door and your heart in ways you've longed to but never knew how—until now."

Holley Gerth, bestselling author of *You're Already Amazing*
and life coach

"We all want to make a difference in others' lives, but so often we miss the opportunity right in front of us. *Reach Out, Gather In* is a compelling invitation to engage with the people who are a part of our every day and watch how God can use our simple acts of kindness to change a life! The best part? Karen Ehman has lived this way of life for years, and now she is showing us how we can too."

Ruth Schwenk, cohost of the *Rootlike Faith* podcast, author of *The Better Mom Devotional*, and co-author of *In a Boat in the Middle of a Lake*

"Karen's voice on hospitality is the mentorship women need. Spiritually rich and readily applicable, *Reach Out, Gather In* is a call to be the evangelist our communities need, simply by opening the door. From our heart attitudes to the practical habits of stocking a guest room, Karen will change your view of hospitality for good."

Phylicia Masonheimer, national bestselling author

"Karen Ehman shares her gift of hospitality in this practical yet encouraging book. *Reach Out, Gather In* is a step-by-step guide for those of us who want to create space where others feel welcomed and loved. Whether in your heart or in your home, this book will motivate you to discover your gifts and share them with others."

Alli Worthington, author of *Standing Strong: A Woman's Guide to Overcoming Adversity and Living with Confidence*, speaker, and business coach

"Karen mentors us in these pages. She beautifully connects heart and home, practical life and vision. She entertained me, motivated me, and held my hand with her words as I read."

Sara E. Hagerty, bestselling author of *Every Bitter Thing Is Sweet, Unseen,* and *Adore*

"I would read anything Karen Ehman writes. I love her writing that much. Karen is the spiritual big sister we all need from time to time, and this devotional is some of her best wisdom. I also absolutely love the depth through the Greek and Hebrew word study throughout the devotional. This is a must-have!"

Nicki Koziarz, bestselling author and Proverbs 31 speaker

"Karen invites us into the beauty and simplicity of 'soul sharing.' I say simplicity because we tend to overcomplicate hospitality, but Karen's unique and creative approach in *Reach Out, Gather In*, makes it feel not only doable but enjoyable. And oh, let me tell you, the recipes are delectable!"

Jeannie Cunnion, author of *Mom Set Free*

"Karen's warmth and love leaps off of the pages of this book, as she inspires you to reach out and gather others into your home. This book will equip you to take action, as she gives biblical and practical ways to show the love of God to others. Her recipes are an added bonus! They are golden."

Courtney Joseph, author and blogger at WomenLivingWell.org

REACH OUT

gather

IN

REACH OUT

gather

IN

40 DAYS TO OPENING YOUR HEART AND HOME

KAREN EHMAN

BETHANYHOUSE
a division of Baker Publishing Group
Minneapolis, Minnesota

© 2020 by Karen Ehman

Published by Bethany House Publishers
11400 Hampshire Avenue South
Bloomington, Minnesota 55438
www.bethanyhouse.com

Bethany House Publishers is a division of
Baker Publishing Group, Grand Rapids, Michigan

Printed in the United States of America

ISBN 978-0-7642-3795-9

Unless otherwise indicated, Scripture quotations are from the Christian Standard Bible®, copyright © 2017 by Holman Bible Publishers. Used by permission. Christian Standard Bible® and CSB® are federally registered trademarks of Holman Bible Publishers.

Scripture quotations identified ESV are from The Holy Bible, English Standard Version® (ESV®), copyright © 2001 by Crossway, a publishing ministry of Good News Publishers. Used by permission. All rights reserved. ESV Text Edition: 2016

Scripture quotations identified NIV are from the Holy Bible, New International Version®. NIV®. Copyright © 1973, 1978, 1984, 2011 by Biblica, Inc.™ Used by permission of Zondervan. All rights reserved worldwide. www.zondervan.com. The "NIV" and "New International Version" are trademarks registered in the United States Patent and Trademark Office by Biblica, Inc.™

Cover design by Kara Klontz
Interior design by William Overbeeke
Interior art by Sarah Rudkin

Author is represented by Meredith Brock at The Brock Agency.

20 21 22 23 24 25 26   7 6 5 4 3 2

to Macey,
For loving our son almost
as much as she loves Jesus

Contents

Find Me Somebody to Love

Discovering Your Niche

Meet Their Needs

Refresh Their Souls

Hospitality Outside the Home

Whose Eyes Do You Have?

Introduction

i, friend,

With the recent need for social distancing, I quickly discovered that one of the simple activities I missed most was being able to sit in person with someone, sharing a steaming cup of something delicious while also sharing life together. I know this up-close human interaction is a delight I will no longer take for granted.

Today, I so wish you and I were in person together sharing a cup of apple cinnamon herbal tea. Why that particular beverage? Because it was over a cup of this tea, poured for me by a woman named Pat, that I began my walk with God. But this isn't a book about Pat. Or tea. Or me. Or even you.

This book is about Jesus and the people in your life he is longing to reach through you. Those whom you see every day, and those who are there, but you just haven't noticed—yet.

But this is more than a book. It's a challenge—part devotional, part guidebook. Together we will explore not only the "how" of hospitality, but the "why." Over forty days (designed to be eight weeks of weekdays only), we will study Scripture, take actionable steps, pray, read real-life examples of hospitality, get our homes ready, try new recipes, and journal our excursions.

I hear from women regularly who wish they were able to creatively love and practically encourage others in their lives. What is holding them back? Yep. You guessed it. They are busy! Holding down jobs. Raising children. Volunteering in their community. Involved in churches and communities. Sounds familiar, doesn't it?

Although you possess a jam-packed schedule, I suspect you also possess a desire to connect with others more deeply, face-to-face and even within the four walls of your home. You may dream of being a world-changer, making your presence really count in the lives of others as you build community with them. The trouble is, you don't know where—or how—to start.

In decades past, using the home and food to show love to others seemed to come naturally; it was woven into the very fiber of a woman's day. But since women today are not necessarily near their kitchens all day long, this assignment can be more challenging.

That's where *Reach Out, Gather In* comes in.

I myself am a mother of three children who has many opportunities for loving, hosting, and feeding people. My mid-century dining-room table is a magnet, attracting many of my children's friends, who hang out at our house or sometimes stop by on their lunch hour to see if they can score a bowl of leftover corn chowder instead of heading for fast-food row. My calendar includes opportunities for taking food to our life group, dropping by a batch of muffins to the teachers' lounge, or making a Crock-Pot of pineapple barbecue pork sandwiches and a platter of apple blondies to welcome the new family who just moved into our neighborhood. As for long-term guests, we've hosted teens and adults for a day—or a year—as they moved into our home and naturally blended into our family.

I've surely made some mistakes. And I've learned a lesson or two along the way. But I hold fast to the truth that God calls us to a life of hospitality, welcoming others into our ordinary lives so they might better know our glorious God.

I'm thrilled you've come along for the challenge. Know that I am cheering you on! My prayer is that by the time you close this book, you will be equipped and inspired. I believe that, by taking this challenge, your home and life will transform into a place where the Gospel is displayed, drawing others closer to Christ and making a difference for eternity.

May God bless you as you open your heart and home to others.

Karen

WHY *Welcome?*

day 1

Holy Leftovers
and Apple Cinnamon Tea

I met Jesus over a cup of apple cinnamon herbal tea.

Oh, I don't mean that he and I sat down in the flesh at the local coffeehouse and sipped on hot beverages served in earthenware mugs, purchased with a buy-one-get-one coupon I pulled out of my purse that was about to expire. I mean that a cup of spiced tea—served to me by a believer with a heart of hospitality in her oh-so-ordinary home— was the means God used to draw me to himself, setting in motion my spiritual walk of faith.

I was a sixteen-year-old junior in high school when a new family moved in just across the road. Their white ranch-style house nestled up next to the country church that stood guard over the four-corner Midwestern intersection I called home. The wife was a stay-at-home mom of two small children, who also headed up the church's youth group. Her husband was the newly hired preacher. She first noticed me outside in my front yard, tossing a softball up in the air all by myself. Miss Pat made it her mission to get to know me.

She invited me to hang out at her home on weekdays when I was finished with my after-school activities. There wasn't a fuss made. No pulling out of all the stops to impress my teenaged self. She simply invited me to pull up a chair and join in the daily happenings of her very commonplace life.

She would pour me a steaming hot cup of apple cinnamon tea and offer me a snack—often fashioned from leftovers from her family's supper the evening before. At this house, I felt welcomed and safe. This led to something even more crucial—I felt loved and known. She took time to get to know the real me, not just the public me—an overachiever whose list of accomplishments and activities was the longest in my entire class of nearly six hundred students. She instead unearthed the private me—a lonely young woman who was sorely unsure of herself, desperate for attention and affirmation.

Since she'd already picked up on the fact that I liked to play softball, she invited me not only to attend youth group but also to be part of the church's softball team. Through her invites I became instantly connected to this pint-sized church with a humongous heart. Soon I was told the Gospel story. How Christ took my place on the cross, paying the penalty for my sin and purchasing my way to heaven. Oh, I had been told the story many times before by my mother, who was a believer. But up until that time, for me Jesus stayed conveniently closed up in the pages of the Bible that sat upon my shelf, only occasionally coming out in my mind at Christmas and Eastertime.

Then, after a few months of attending that church, I responded to the Spirit's invitation and placed my trust in Jesus at a youth retreat campfire one September Saturday night.

My life has never been the same.

God can use anything and anyone. He has no limits. He can—and often does—use a flawlessly presented worship experience—one that rivals the most elaborately orchestrated concert—to beckon someone to himself. He can reach a lost or weary soul through a television show or radio broadcast. He might pique a person's interest in spiritual matters through the written word on the pages of a book or pamphlet. But I find that—most often—the Lord uses everyday relationships to expand his kingdom.

I once took an impromptu poll of the people in my Bible study group, asking them how they first came to faith. Of the nearly thirty people in attendance, all but one had first responded to the Gospel and made a decision to become a Christ-follower because of a relationship with someone in their everyday life. (One person had begun their walk with God due to listening to Christian radio.) For some it was a neighbor, co-worker, or other person they personally knew. For others it was a stranger-turned-friend who first opened their heart—and often their home—to them as they naturally shared about their relationship with Christ. These people gave them a front-row seat in their ordinary life. There they observed God intricately involved in the daily life of a human in a captivating way that made them want a relationship with him too.

The New Testament is full of accounts of people coming to faith. In 1 Thessalonians, we catch a very important fact about this phenomenon. Lives were not transformed solely because information about Jesus was shared—although there is no doubt that information about the Gospel is required. A catalyst for the conversion is tucked away in chapter 2, where we find Paul talking about the spiritual growth of those he loved who comprised this early church congregation.

> Just as a nursing mother cares for her children, so we cared for you. Because we loved you so much, we were delighted to share with you not only the gospel of God but our lives as well.
>
> 1 Thessalonians 2:7–8 NIV

Did you catch it? They shared not only their words. They shared their very lives.

In the original Greek language in which the New Testament was written, the word rendered *lives* doesn't just denote the happenings in the course of someone's day. It goes further. The word used, *psuché*, is derived from the root word *psyxō*, which means "to breathe, blow."[1]

Does it make you think of any English words? If you guessed *psyche* or *psychology*, you are correct. This word encapsulates what we know as the human soul (or psyche). It refers to one's distinctive personality or unique personhood. It is who someone is at their very core.

As we, like the apostle Paul, open our hearts, connecting our souls with another's through the sharing of life, we create a safe space where the Gospel can be displayed, and God's table expanded. Others can come to know Christ through this simple soul sharing.

Soul sharing isn't as complicated as we make it out to be. It needn't be expensive. Or labor-intensive. It isn't fancy or flashy. What is it, then?

Soul sharing is caring for the deepest part of another as you share with them your material possessions—as well as your time—in a way that points them to Jesus. It is how the family of God welcomes another.

And, it reminds us of those who have paved the way before us, inviting us to share in the Gospel as well. It is the most exciting of commonplace adventures that results in lives affected for eternity.

Are you ready to watch God work, fetching souls and knitting them to himself? If so, then fire up the stove, put the teakettle on, and watch with eager anticipation for whomever God sends your way.

My ONE-SENTENCE PRAYER
FOR THE WEEK

At the beginning of each section of this book, you will be asked to write a one-sentence prayer for the week, encapsulating what you hope to learn and apply. Go ahead and do so for day one in the space provided below, asking God to help you catch a passion for soul sharing.

day 2

But Do I Have To?

ut, Mom, do I *have* to?" Boy, did my kids utter those words hundreds of times over the years! Whether it was when I announced it was time to do their schoolwork, tidy up their bedrooms, or pile in the Buick to go somewhere, they sometimes pushed back, testing whether what I had just instructed them to do was optional or actually obligatory. Usually it was the latter.

There are numerous subjects that present themselves in the pages of Scripture that evoke a similar response from us as believers. When we read Jesus' admonition in Luke 6:27 to "love your enemies," our immediate thought may be, "Are ya crazy?" In that same passage—part of the famous Sermon on the Mount—we are also instructed in verse 28 to bless those who curse us. Uh . . . blessing them isn't exactly what we had in mind. And then we read these words in 1 Peter 4:9–10:

> Be hospitable to one another without complaining. Just as each one has received a gift, use it to serve others, as good stewards of the varied grace of God.

Be hospitable. But it is so much work! And quite a bit of hassle. It interrupts my plans and cramps what little style I may have.

But the Bible is one step ahead of us. As if anticipating the grumbling rolling around in our brains and eventually emitting from our lips, it overlays it with a little caveat: *without complaining.*

Busted.

When met with our choruses of "But, Jesus, do I *have* to?" the resounding answer is yes. First Peter 4:9 isn't a sweet suggestion. We aren't told to think about maybe opening our hearts and homes sometime. You know, in case one day we happen to feel like it. First Peter 4:9 not only assumes that we will offer hospitality but tells us how we are to do it: no griping allowed.

The word translated as "complaining" (or in some Bible versions as "grumbling") is the Greek word *goggysmós*. It cracked me up the first time I saw that word printed in the English transliteration. No matter how I tried to pronounce it, I couldn't. And each stab I took at it sounded just like the concept it was meant to portray. It sounds like a person grumbling and protesting, mumbling their immense annoyance.

Actually, this term doesn't just refer to our audible complaints about an action we are asked to perform. It carries the concept of secrecy too—of muttering and murmuring under our breath, expressing a secret displeasure that is not openly asserted. The contrast of such a cantankerous attitude is to perform a task joyfully, with a cheerful mind and disposition.

I think the concept of hospitality is often misunderstood. When you think of the word *hospitality*, what comes to mind?

Entertaining in your perfectly cleaned home, complete with stunning, high-end décor?

A gourmet meal that rivals something straight out of a Food Network special?

A formal invitation with a planned-out menu and carefully thought-out conversation starters?

The biblical concept of hospitality is straightforward in its definition. The original word is *philoxenos*. It is a combination of two other words: *philos* and *xenos*. *Philos* means love, and *xenos* means stranger. Hospitality is simply loving strangers and continuing to love them until the strangers become friends. There is no mention of a menu, no talk of home design.

I would run out of fingers and toes if I tried to use them to count all of the former strangers who are now my friends. These souls I got to know by inviting them over to our home—or I became acquainted with them by being hospitable somewhere other than within my four walls. (More ideas on that coming later!)

Stranger love isn't the only aspect of hospitality. Scripture also tethers this topic to loving fellow believers in passages such as Romans 12:13 and Romans 16:23. Hospitality is a tool we can use to serve those we barely know or to minister to our closest friends. And it can be a powerful means of building up those in our local church as we offer our homes as venues where our spiritual community can flourish and care for each other.

Today, let's take some time to think through how this command of offering hospitality fits into your life. And—if you are up for it—take the challenge to memorize a verse that pertains to this important practice in the life of a follower of Christ.

Record your responses in the spaces provided. For the memory verse, turn to page 249, where all of the suggested memory verses have been designed for you and are ready to be utilized to help you cement the verses in your mind, write them on your heart, and then live them out.

Ponder AND Pray

Before reading this day's entry, how would you have defined the word *hospitality*?

_____

_____

_____

Knowing now that the chief concept of biblical hospitality is the love of strangers, have you ever been the recipient of such love by someone you barely knew welcoming you into their home? Describe it here.

_____

_____

_____

What keeps you from opening your own home to others, especially those you don't know very well? List as many reasons (dare I say excuses?) as you can below.

_____

_____

_____

Study AND Store

Memory Verse 1

Be *hospitable* to one another without complaining. Just as each one has received a *gift*, use it to serve others, as good stewards of the varied grace of *God*.

1 PETER 4:9-10

day 3
Open Your Gift
(and Then Give It Away!)

I can hardly wait for the white-elephant gift exchange my father's side of the family has as a tradition on Christmas Eve each year. Guests at this wacky party draw numbers out of a basket. Then they proceed in numerical order to open up one of the goofy wrapped gifts they have each brought for the occasion. What a blast it is to see what outlandish present each person gets, usually snagged at a secondhand store or yard sale.

But seeing the zany presents—perhaps a neon purple planter shaped like an owl, or a relic gizmo or gadget from an infomercial of decades past—isn't the only fun part. Things start getting really exciting—and in our family, sometimes even intense—when people are allowed to "steal" someone else's gift based on what number they drew.

Our family has gotten a bit cutthroat when stealing some of the items over the years. Not content with what they opened, they instead desired whatever object was deemed to be the zaniest of that year's collection.

Each of us as believers has been fashioned by God in a unique way, complete with natural talents and spiritual gifts. Sometimes it is tempting to look at somebody else with their unique package of strengths and abilities and wish that we possessed it.

I know I've spent way too much time wishing I had someone else's gifting. Sometimes I wished for a natural knack they had. I remember one woman in particular who was so fabulous at all things crafty. She could sew. She made her own greeting cards. She could take raw materials that were lying around the house and whip up something that was not only functional, but beautiful as well. I, on the other hand, do not have an ounce of crafter's blood coursing through my veins. Why, my own children knew better than to bring me a badge to sew onto their uniforms when they were younger. I would reach for the hot-glue gun! In our house, Dad was the master seamstress.

In time, through the encouragement of some older Christians who listened to my struggles with gift envy, I finally came to the place where I decided to discover—and then be content with—my specific wiring when it came to natural talents and spiritual gifts. How freeing this was! Rather than looking at one of my siblings in Christ, longing to do ministry the way they did, I instead embarked on an exciting journey, observing God use me as he touched the lives of others.

Our focus verse for this section (which I have encouraged you to memorize, if you have time) is 1 Peter 4:9–10: "Be hospitable to one another without complaining. Just as each one has received a gift, use it to serve others, as good stewards of the varied grace of God." We've already discussed being hospitable without grousing about it. Today, let's focus on verse 10 in this passage, which talks about each of us receiving a gift.

What is the purpose of that gift? Is it so we can pat ourselves on the back for having it? Nope. The gift really isn't given for our benefit. Look again at what it says: . . . **"use it to serve others."**

You are not the intended recipient of your gift. The people in your life are. Your gift is a tool God will use to serve others, building them up and helping them to find their place in his kingdom.

The original word *gift* in this passage is the Greek word *charisma*. This noun, in essence, denotes an endowment of grace intended to edify the church, a Holy Spirit–powered service to the body of believers to carry out God's plan for his people. Verse 10 also implies that we don't all have identical gifts. There is nothing matchy-matchy about the ways we serve. We are stewards of "the varied grace of God." The word *varied* here in the original language is *poikilos*—perhaps my favorite word of this verse. It means—wait for it—many-colored, diverse, and manifold.

Okay, perhaps the word *manifold* threw you. I myself don't have a whole lot of knowledge of this word. I remember singing the hymn "Great Is Thy Faithfulness" that has a line that states "join with all nature in manifold witness." I surmised that manifold meant many . . . maybe?

Additionally, because my husband, my son, my brother, and my stepbrother all build cars for a living, I know there is a car part called a manifold. Maybe its definition can help shed some light on this concept. It is:

> A system of pipes that divides a flow and carries it to more than one place or that brings a flow from a number of places to a single place.[1]

What an accurate depiction of what our gifts do for the family of God! When we divide, we maximize, carrying the love of God to more than one place, compounding the impact we have on the lives of those within our sphere of influence.

This makes me think about the concept of being fishers of people, which is how Jesus referred to us in Matthew 4:19: "'Follow me,' he told them, 'and I will make you fish for people.'"

I have a tad bit of experience with fishing. My aunt and uncle live on a lake, and their entire family—kids and grandkids included—are avid fishers. I know from watching them that you don't use the same bait for every species of fish. You mix it up: Red worms for catching trout. Leeches for luring walleye. Minnows for snagging largemouth bass. (Why am I suddenly craving a fish sandwich with extra tartar sauce?)

In real life, we are to fish for people. Therefore, we also need to mix it up when it comes to what will lure them to Christ. God, in his infinite wisdom, knows exactly what type of people will be drawn to his heart through the gifts, abilities, and resources each of us possesses.

Make it your aim not only to discover, but to embrace and then use your gifts.

Ponder AND Pray

Time to focus on your distinctive wiring. Each of us has natural abilities and talents, along with spiritual gifts. God will use the beautiful package that is you to reach others, whether they are already believers or have yet to hear the good news of the Gospel. Take a few moments to work through the following questions, designed to help you pinpoint these qualities you already possess.

Has there ever been a time when someone commented on a natural ability you have? What was it? How did it make you feel when they pointed out that you possess this quality?

_____

_____

_____

What passions do you have that God could use to serve others? Examples: You enjoy caring for children; you are skilled at painting and hanging wallpaper; you are an efficient house cleaner or a tremendous cook; you are an excellent gardener or automotive mechanic. List three to five passions or hobbies that could be used to serve others in the space below.

_____

_____

_____

_____

_____

Now, have you ever explored what spiritual gift you might possess? (You will find these gifts listed in the Bible in the following passages: Romans 12:6-8 and 1 Corinthians 12:4-11, 28.) Flip open your Bible—or tap your way if you use a digital form of Scripture—and read through these passages. Record any initial thoughts about these gifts below.

What experience do you have with spiritual gifts? Have you ever made a concerted effort to discover which ones you have? If so, list the gift or gifts you have below. (If not, check out the resources section on page 246 to see my go-to sites and books on the topic.)

TAKE ROOT *and* TAKE ACTION

Look back over the section above. Identify one of the qualities that make up your unique personality. It could be a natural ability, passion, hobby, or spiritual gift. Below, write a goal that pertains to this gift. For example, "I want to be more deliberate to use my love of cooking to serve others in my life who are dealing with medical issues or are hurting or grieving."

Remember, your gift is God's grace, scattered about to reach others for his glory.

day 4
Clutter-Busting Basics

*a*re you ready to learn to live a life of welcome, using your gifts and talents—along with your home—to love and serve others? Or is there a little bit of hesitation when it comes to the whole subject of your home? I mean, you would gladly have others over for a meal, that is, if you actually could see the top of your dining-room table! Or maybe you have killer dust bunnies under your sofa and you're slightly concerned they may bite your guests in the ankles. Time for a little lesson on decluttering your house. (Then, in the next section, we will tackle cleaning.)

Let's start with those pesky piles. Oh, I know you have them. We all do! Piles of paper, piles of assorted kitchen clutter, piles of wayward items that have yet to find a home. Do you know what all of those piles are? They are the result of two little words that are unfortunately ingrained into your vocabulary. Those two awful words are . . .

"For now."

You know, "I'll lay this mail and these newspaper ads here *for now."*

"I'll place these clean towels I haven't found time to fold yet over there *for now.*"

"I don't know what to do with all of this _____ (fill in the blank), so I'll plop it here *for now.*"

Friends, our *for nows* are wrecking us! You must realize that every pile in your place is a stack of unmade decisions. Your brain was too overloaded to decide where the item should go, so you just *for nowed* it and went on your merry—and messy—way.

For many of us, the problem isn't just where to put the stuff. It is also that we have too much of it! So, first let's learn to do a little de-junking, ridding ourselves of unnecessary objects. Make a vow that for the next six weeks you will devote a chunk of time each week to decluttering. The result? Fewer piles and more smiles. Here's how:

First, you'll need five boxes, bins, or laundry baskets. They will hold items you come across that belong somewhere other than where they are at the moment.

Label the first box **Put Back**. Inside of it place another small lidded container such as a shoe box or plastic tote. This box will be used to collect the items that are out of place in your home. The smaller container will hold items such as pens, bobby pins, and coins so they don't get lost in the bigger box.

The second box is denoted **Take Back**. This will corral all of those items in your home that don't belong to you and need to be returned somewhere. You know, library books, a shoe from your son's friend who spent the night last week, a pan from the sweet lady at church who made your family brownies two months ago, etc.

The third box will be used for garbage. Label it **Toss**. Line it with a garbage bag so that when it becomes full, you can tie it up and transport it to the trash can. If you are a family that recycles, you can also have a box or bin for that purpose to hold paper, glass, and metal objects.

Next, you'll want to have a box for those items that are still in good shape, but are no longer needed or wanted at your home. Label this one **Charity** or **Garage Sale**. If you will donate your belongings to a charity or homeless shelter, as a box fills up, seal it and put it in your vehicle to be ready to drop off the next time you are near a donation center.

The last box in the bunch will be labeled **Nostalgia**. (More on this in a minute.)

Determine that you will be ruthless. If you have not used it, needed it (but couldn't find it), worn it, or enjoyed looking at it in the past year—then you're going to give it the old heave-ho!

Haul your boxes into your least problematic room. (You don't want to overwhelm yourself.) Beginning in one corner of the room, pick up an article, and ask yourself the following five questions:

1. Is this item out of place? Place it in the *Put Back* box.
2. Does this item need to be returned to someone or somewhere? Into the *Take Back* box it goes.
3. Is this item in such dire shape that it is no longer usable? Place it in the *Toss* box. If it is made of metal, glass, paper, or plastic, it goes in the recycle bin if you are going to add this step.
4. Is this item in fine shape but no longer needed by anyone in our family? Put it in the *Charity* or *Garage Sale* box.
5. Now here is the final question: Is this item no longer needed by anyone in our family, but one of them is so attached to it that if I pitch it now, they'll be emotionally damaged for life and someday will be seen in an online viral video crying over my cruel actions?

Then into the *Nostalgia* box it goes. All your kiddos can have a few nostalgia boxes with favorite "keeper" items. I like to attach a note to the item such as, "You wouldn't fall asleep without this stuffed turtle by your side."

Once your question-and-answer exercise is finished, look down in your hand. Is the item still there? Then it must be:

A. Something you actually want or need and . . .
B. It must be in the proper room of the house.

Continue making a sweep around the entire room, following the same procedure with each item you encounter. Check every drawer, shelf, and closet.

Crank up some music you enjoy or listen to a podcast or an audiobook to help the time pass more quickly. Having a friend also helps; you can take turns helping each other de-junk.

Now, with what is left, you need to think logically. Just having things looking neat does not necessarily mean they are arranged in a user-friendly manner. You want to place items back according to their frequency of use. No sense having a bunch of kitchen gadgets you never use in a drawer right by the stove and the measuring cups you do use way across the room.

Taking time to de-clutter and then rethink your work patterns will lead to an organized and functional home. You can do it!

Happy organizing!

It's high time you booted that clutter to the gutter so you'll feel more confident having others over to your home—and actually have space for them to sit! Work through this section and then roll up your sleeves and get started. This is clutter's last stand!

························· **MY CLUTTER-BUSTING PLAN** ·················

The greatest source of clutter in my home is (circle one):

- Paper
- Undone work such as laundry to be put away
- Kids' items
- Items that are in the wrong room
- I just own too much stuff and some of it needs to go!
- _____ (Other—fill in the blank)

One action I need to take in order to stop junk from piling up in the first place is to:

_____

_____

_____

Now, in two or three sentences, write out your goals in the area of de-junking. Do you long to have your living room be a place where you can actually live rather than a catchall of clutter? Do you want to cease stacking the papers in your life all over your dwelling? Are you ready to design a plan for keeping your kids' items organized and out of the way? Use the space below to write at least one goal you have:

_____

_____

_____

_____

_____

_____

Lastly, commit to a specific time for de-junking your home:

I will make the rounds, gathering the items I no longer want or

need. I will do this on _____ .

(Example: the first Saturday of every month)

A Fresh Take on Leftovers

I have such fond memories of time spent at my mentor Miss Pat's house, sitting at her kitchen table, grabbing a bite to eat as she informally discipled me. It never bothered me that sometimes she fed me reheated leftovers. The welcoming atmosphere made even the humblest of fare more than enough for a delightful dining experience.

Below are some ideas for infusing new life into your leftovers, transforming them into delicious paninis. Serve them with a handful of chopped raw veggies and some fruit. Even drop-in guests will have a tasty meal. Remember, don't try to impress others with your fancy foods; bless them instead with your loving presence.

Five Fabulous Paninis from Leftovers

These lightly grilled sandwich combos have one thing in common: They all start with a leftover from dinner as their main ingredient. Throw some together when unexpected company winds up in your kitchen along with an appetite. For all of them, a suggested bread is given, but feel free to switch it up, using whatever loaf you have on hand. The key is using an artisan loaf, not a cheap grocery store variety. Instructions are given for using a frying pan, but you may also use a panini-press electric grill.

Chicken Pesto Caprese

For each sandwich:

Two slices artisan sourdough bread
Mayonnaise
Fresh basil leaves (or you may substitute pesto paste)
Fresh mozzarella cheese, thinly sliced
Leftover cooked chicken breast
Sliced tomato
Italian dressing
Fresh ground sea salt
Black pepper
Butter, softened

To assemble:

Spread a thin coat of mayonnaise on one slice of bread. With the mayonnaise side up, top with a few basil leaves, some fresh mozzarella cheese and then some sliced chicken. Place a slice of tomato on top of the chicken. Lightly drizzle the tomato with Italian dressing and sprinkle with ground sea salt and black pepper, to taste. Place on a few more slices of mozzarella and two or three basil leaves. Spread mayonnaise on the second slice of sourdough bread and place on top of the sandwich.

In a frying pan, melt some butter over medium heat. Place the sandwich in the pan, then spread softened butter on the exposed bread. Grill, watching very carefully and flipping when lightly golden brown. Sandwich is ready when the cheese is slightly melted. Serve warm.

Grainy Mustard Ham, Apple, and Swiss

For each sandwich:

Two slices artisan marble rye bread
Whole-grain mustard
Two thin slices Swiss cheese
3-4 slices Granny Smith apple, sliced very thin
One thick slice of leftover ham
Butter, softened

To assemble:

Spread a thin coat of mustard on one slice of bread. Top the bread, mustard side up, with a piece of Swiss cheese, the apple slices, followed by the ham. Place second slice of cheese on top of the ham. Spread more mustard on the second slice of bread and place it on top of the sandwich.

In a frying pan, melt some butter over medium heat. Place the sandwich in the pan, then spread softened butter on the exposed bread. Cook, watching very carefully and flipping when lightly golden brown. Serve warm.

Apricot Turkey-Bacon Delight

For each sandwich:

Two slices artisan ciabatta bread
Two slices Muenster or provolone cheese
Arugula leaves
Peach preserves
One slice bacon, cooked crisp (I use nitrate-free turkey bacon.)
A few slices of leftover cooked turkey
Butter, softened

To assemble:

Place a slice of cheese on top of the first slice of bread. Lay on a few leaves of arugula. Top with 2 tablespoons of the peach preserves. Tear the bacon into two or three pieces and place on top of the preserves. Place the turkey on the sandwich, followed by more arugula and the second piece of cheese. Place second piece of bread on top.

In a frying pan, melt some butter over medium heat. Place the sandwich in the pan, then spread softened butter on the exposed bread. Grill, watching very carefully and flipping when lightly golden brown and cheese is melted. Serve warm.

Mexicali Meatloaf

For each sandwich:

    Two slices artisan multigrain bread
    Two slices sharp cheddar cheese
    One or two slices leftover meatloaf, ½ inch thick
    Salsa, mild or medium
    Canned jalapeño slices, optional
    Butter, softened

To assemble:

Place a slice of cheese on top of the first slice of bread. Top with meatloaf. Spoon on some salsa and place a few jalapeño slices on top, if you dare. Add the second slice of cheese and finish with the remaining slice of bread.

In a frying pan, melt some butter over medium heat. Place the sandwich in the pan, then spread softened butter on the exposed bread. Grill, watching very carefully and flipping when lightly golden brown and the cheese is melted. Serve warm.

FAMILY *First,* BUT NOT *Family* ONLY

day 6

Relatively Speaking

I love my family. They are the most important humans to me on earth. Sure, we have our share of dysfunction. We sometimes disagree over politics. Other times we fight over the most trivial of things. I mean, come on—who really cares if the proper name of the summertime insect that flickers at dusk is *lightning bug* or *firefly*? (This dispute is quickly settled when our always-researching, creature-loving son corrects us all, informing us that the proper entomological name is *lampyridae*.)

I've spent oodles of time serving my family. I've spent countless hours on my knees—and sometimes flat on my face—praying for them and about situations in their lives. There isn't anyone on earth I would rather spend time with. However, as much as I love my family, they can easily morph into something they were never intended to be.

An idol.

An idol is anything we put before God. We pay more attention to it. We seek its approval. We spend too much time on it. Usually, we might think of earthly idols as work or an overemphasis on a hobby or passion. Material possessions and money certainly can become idols. But, when we place our families on a pedestal and spend all our energies on making them happy, catering to their every whim, we make of them an idol.

But placing the human beings in our clan before God is only half the problem of this practice. The other hitch is that, if we spend all our efforts on our family, we won't have margin in our schedules for being involved in the lives of those to whom we are not related.

A read through Scripture will show that God cares greatly about being inclusive of those with whom we are not physically—or legally—related. In fact, that is how he treats us!

God adopted us as his own. Ephesians 1:5 states, "He predestined us to be adopted as sons through Jesus Christ for himself, according to the good pleasure of his will." And this wasn't because of our stellar behavior. While we were still sinners, Christ died for us (Romans 5:8). And then he adopted us, folding us into his royal family.

So many familial terms are used in Scripture. God is referred to as our Father. He calls us his children. We are mentioned as being siblings, and Scripture refers to us as brother or sister. God's example of knitting together those who are not related by blood is a model for us to emulate. It will not lessen the love we have for our family members if we open wide the circle, making room for more people in our hearts and homes. In fact, it will serve as a wonderful example to our loved ones who are watching.

If we parents want to raise children who are others-centered and ministry-minded, we must lead by example. How in the world can we expect our children to live lives of hospitality if they never see us doing it? If we only spend our time pampering them, and catering to their every whim, we risk raising selfish children.

Oh, I'm not saying there isn't a time to spoil your family. Or that there are never occasions to spend time with just those in your immediate crew. But what I am saying is that we should rethink those times of celebration for us. They might also be times of loneliness for others. While you may be relishing the company of your loved ones, someone else might be home, staring at their four walls, all alone and lonely.

Although we are alive in this time of social media and "friends," experts assert that—even though we are over-connected digitally—we are lonelier now than ever.

Psalm 68:6 (NIV) states, "God sets the lonely in families." Notice that it doesn't just say that God comforts the lonely. He certainly does that directly and through the power of Scripture. However, he allows us the privilege of being people who throw our arms wide open and welcome in a hurting soul so they know someone else on earth actually cares.

Over the last decade, our house has often bustled with activity. Teenage boys slept in our basement family room, spending the night after a baseball or football game. A squad of girls from the volleyball team devoured more bottles of ranch dressing and orders of cheesy breadsticks than I care to count. As the kids grew older, cars would be lined up and down our street as our house became a hangout for teenagers of driving age. Our grocery bill soared. My time spent cleaning increased. But I would not trade those days for anything.

God prompted me to view these years through a lens of ministry. I came to love many of these teenagers as my own, and several of them to this day still have me in their phone contact list as "Mom E." As I served endless bowls of cheesy corn chowder and pan after pan of peanut butter apple crisp, I leaned in and listened. I got to know more about these teens than just their names and what type of dressing they liked on their salad. I got to know them as people.

Some of them were from wonderful homes, with caring, loving parents and lots of support academically and in life. Others were from situations that broke my heart. It was as if they had started out in the race of life already way behind the starting line. They had no one to advocate for them or to help them with their college or job applications. They were figuring out life on their own—some not having much success at it.

These kids became our kids. My husband and I naturally folded them into our family life. One, who was on the brink of becoming homeless, even lived with us for six months so he could graduate from high school. I don't say this because we always had an exemplary attitude. Sometimes we didn't. I say this because living this way became a habit—a hard habit to break. Soon it was not a foreign concept to include others around our Thanksgiving table or beside our tree at Christmastime, their own stockings hanging on the mantel next to my children's. It became the norm. And, best of all, we didn't just see hearts cheered—we saw souls saved as lives were changed for eternity.

Just off the top of my head I can think of five young people now walking closely with the Lord who were not back when they were sitting at my kitchen table eating my food. God used our family—hear me now— *despite* our sometimes less-than-wonderful behavior, to welcome them into a home where they felt wanted. And we tried to naturally, and often, share the Gospel with them in both word and deed.

So, as you work your way through this forty-day challenge, of course I hope you will utilize some of the ideas and recipes to spoil and encourage your family members. But don't stop there. Pull up a few more chairs to your table and reach out to those who may be lonely or hurting. Allow God to use you to draw others to himself.

I hope many in your life who currently are not walking with Christ will respond to the Gospel once they've experienced feeling a part of your family, however crazy or calm it may be. (If it is like ours, it is certainly more crazy than calm!)

Below, craft your one-sentence prayer for the week, encapsulating what you hope to learn and apply when it comes to the concept of family first—but not family only.

ONE-SENTENCE PRAYER
FOR THE WEEK

day 7

Don't Just Tell Them—
Show Them

*P*art of what I do as an author and speaker is to help train others who want to get their start writing or speaking. Whether I am standing before a large group at a conference or sharing a cup of coffee with a few others as we chat about these professions, one crucial point I attempt to drive home is this: Whether you are writing content or presenting it verbally in front of a group, don't just tell them—*show them*.

Let me explain what this means.

It's easy to merely relay information and expect your audience to understand what you mean. It's an altogether different thing to creatively convey that same content in a way that evokes the emotions of your audience. Are they simply hearing or seeing the words you are speaking or writing, or are their senses involved? Can they envision the vibrant fall colors of the leaves on the tree you're describing? Do they practically smell the crisp air, slightly steeped in the scent of a roaring bonfire? Can they almost taste the gooey chocolate and marshmallow s'more you have just described? Do their legs nearly itch after experiencing your depiction of the scratchy, wool plaid socks your character is wearing? If they can, you know you have succeeded as a communicator.

This concept is also present in family life. Sure, your family members know you love them. That's presumed. If you have a spouse, they know you stood up and recited your vows, declaring your love for them in front of those in attendance. No doubt if you have children, and they were asked whether you love them, they would surely say you do. Whether you have parents, siblings, cousins, or aunts and uncles, typically they know that they are treasured by you. But do you really show them your love in tangible ways? Do they actually feel your love with all of their senses?

The book of 1 Timothy was penned by the apostle Paul to his younger co-worker Timothy, most likely in the mid-sixties AD during a mission trip we don't find chronicled in Scripture. This journey occurred after the events documented in Acts and somewhere in between Paul's first stay in prison and his final Roman imprisonment. Its main theme is how the Gospel changes our lives in very concrete and definite ways. It also gives advice on how we are to relate to one another.

In chapter five, verse eight, Paul makes this bold assertion:

> But if anyone does not provide for his own family, especially for his own household, he has denied the faith and is worse than an unbeliever.

Over the years I have heard this verse quoted on numerous occasions, mostly referring to taking care of your family financially. Certainly, that is one aspect of what is commanded here. But let's pull back the curtain even further by looking at a few words from this verse in the original language in which they were written. Here are the Greek definitions of four key words:

- *Family*: one's own people; their biological family
- *Household*: domestic, intimate family members, including any servants that reside with them
- *Provide:* to take thought of, think about, respect, and care for
- *Unbeliever:* not faithful; does not always refer to the unconverted but may describe someone who rejects the true faith

So, now that we know what these individual words mean, let's take a stab at stating the broad concept of this verse. Maybe it is this: If anyone does not make it a point to take thought of and care for the family members and others who reside in their own home, then they are not truly living out their faith. It is almost as if they aren't believers at all.

Ouch. Stepped on my own toes with that one.

Are our family members at the forefront of our minds as we go about our days? Of course, as stated earlier, we don't want to make an idol of those in our family, but we do want to have them at the top of our list when it comes to showing love and care. We can't settle for just supposing they know we love them. That there is no need to put in any further effort. No! We need to strive to sincerely show them with our actions that we are completely crazy about them.

Time not just to tell, but to show your family how much they mean to you!

Spend a little time contemplating the following section. Record your responses in the spaces provided. For the memory verse, remember that you can turn to page 249, where all of the suggested memory verses have been designed for you so you can photocopy them and have copies to place in a location where you will be sure to see them often.

Ponder AND Pray

On a scale of one to ten, with one being never and ten being constantly, how often would you say that visibly and tangibly showing love to your family members is a part of your week? Write your number below.

My current number is: _____

How would you like this to change in the future? Write a sentence stating your goals in the area of really showing your immediate family members your love.

_____

_____

_____

What ideas do you have for making this goal become a reality? What actions could you take to convey love to your family? Write any ideas below.

_____

_____

_____

Memory Verse 2

But if anyone does not provide for his own *family*, especially for his own household, he has denied the *faith* and is worse than an unbeliever.

1 TIMOTHY 5:8

day 8

Sticky Notes, Bananas, and a Tank Full of Gas

*M*y husband tells me he loves me several times a month. Oh, I don't mean that he snuggles up next to me on the couch and sweetly whispers in my ear while we are watching *Shark Tank* and splitting a thin-crust veggie pizza, heavy on the sauce, which is our current practice on Friday nights these days. Nope. I hear his sentiment of love loud and clear in a different way.

When I hop in my vehicle and notice that the gas tank is full, and I didn't fill it.

Now, that might not seem like a huge deal, a guy putting gas in his wife's car tank. But for me it speaks volumes. I don't like the smell of gasoline. And I especially don't like standing out in the bitter cold, like it is in Michigan during January (which is when I am currently writing these words. Brrr!). And I for sure don't like when I am on a trip—whether it is across the state or just across town—and I hear that familiar ping, alerting me to the fact that I am almost out of fuel.

My husband knows all of this about me. That is why, ever since we were able to afford a second car for me to drive, he has made sure it has plenty of gas, rarely letting the tank register below half full. If I were only looking for signs of his love in traditional ways—candy, flowers, or his actually verbalizing his love—I might have missed it. But my man tends to show a person he cares by completing tasks for them that help make their life easier.

For me, it might also be doing up the dishes I didn't get to the night before when he gets up at three a.m. to get ready for work. For our son, who recently purchased his first home, it might be going over to help him install an air conditioner or stain his new wood fence. He shows our youngest son love by doing things outdoors with him. They recently went on a father-son hike in the Grand Canyon, using two free airline tickets we had received. And, since our daughter lives several states away, he sometimes takes a few days off work to go down south to her house and tackle the "Daddy Do" list of projects to be done in her mid-century home. And he shows love to his ninety-year-old mother, who lives in an assisted living facility, by making the four-hour round trip some Saturdays just to take her out to lunch at Panera Bread for her favorite sandwich and a hot cup of coffee.

Using words of affection is certainly appropriate and effective. However, showing our love through nonverbal ways, especially acts of service, turns the volume up even more, conveying to our family members our deep love for them. First John 3:18 seems to encourage such behavior.

Little children, let us not love in word or speech, but in action and in truth.

Certainly, this verse isn't proposing that we shouldn't show love verbally. Rather, it is urging us to not stop there. We ought to also convey
our true feelings by backing them up with actions. You might complete
a family member's chore for them on a particularly busy day when they
are tight on time. Or maybe you could run an errand for them such as
dropping something off at the dry cleaners or picking up a library book.
Any action that speaks love to them.

Over the years, for me this has meant dozens—if not hundreds—of
sticky notes I've left in my children's schoolbooks and folders, in my
husband's lunch pail, or on a mirror somewhere in the house, accom-
panied by a little gift. Sometimes I even took a ballpoint pen and wrote
a message of love on a banana before tucking it in someone's lunch bag
for the day. My sticky-note sentiments were coupled with homemade
goodies, or maybe a little treat or trinket I had picked up for them when
I was out and about shopping.

Are you ready to love your loved ones not just with your spoken words
but by springing into action?

Love in word. But also, love in deed. This will indeed convey your
love to your family. (See what I did right there?)

Take a few moments to work through the following questions, designed to help you brainstorm a few ideas for showing love—and dishing
out a heaping dose of hospitality—to your own family members this
week.

Ponder AND *Pray*

Today, let's take a little inventory of our family members, formulating some possible actions that will speak even louder than our words. Fill in the following chart and then answer the questions below it.

In the blanks below, list the members of your immediate family. (If you need more blanks, you can also do this exercise in a journal or on a piece of paper.)

Name:

Action:

Name:

Action:

Name:

Action:

Name:

Action:

Name:

Action:

Name:

Action:

In the space after each name, jot down at least one action you think would speak love to them. Try to crawl into their brain and get specific, recording something that you might not enjoy, but that they would be touched by.

TAKE ROOT and TAKE ACTION

So that this is not just an exercise in thinking—but one that requires action—look over the list of people above. Whip out your calendar app on your phone—or your paper calendar—and write the name of each family member on the first day of different months in the next year. Then, when you see their name pop up at the beginning of the month, follow through with your good intentions by performing one of the actions of love sometime during their assigned month.

day 9
Quickstep Cleaning

*a*s we prepare to live a life of welcome, opening both our hearts and homes to others, we may get a little apprehensive about the whole opening-our-homes gig. On day four in the last section, we kicked our clutter to the gutter. Now let's tackle the regular housecleaning that must be done.

Not a fan of cleaning? Find it rather unpleasant? When something is unpleasant, we want to get it over with fast. Anyone taking out a splinter or ripping off a bandage knows this. The same goes for tasks. Cleaning is often unlikable work. So, let's get it over with—and fast! It's time you learned the latest domestic dance craze, quickstep cleaning.

I first discovered this concept fifteen years ago when I read a book called *Speed Cleaning* by Jeff Campbell. It revolutionized my weekly cleaning and gained me white space in my schedule.

Here is how it works:

First, have the home relatively de-junked. This isn't the time to be putting away junk mail, stray electronics, homeless toys, or laundry piled on a table. You need to be able to actually get to the surfaces you want to clean!

Utilize the proper tools and have them on you as you clean. You can do this with the help of an apron. You may want to purchase a speed-cleaning apron online from thecleanteam.com. Or, easily make your own by sewing a loop of cord to each side of a carpenter's apron designed to hold nails. This way, you can place rags and sponges in the pockets on the front of the apron and can hang a spray bottle on each hip in the loops of cord. This apron empowers you! You'll only need to walk the perimeter of your home ONCE instead of several times, since you will have all your tools and products on you.

Hang glass cleaner on one loop and all-purpose cleaner on the other. In the pockets put rags, sponges, wood polish, scouring powder, a toothbrush, a plastic scraper, etc. And in your back jeans pocket or waistband? An ostrich feather duster. (Don't get a chicken-feather one. They are cheap. They don't work. Ostrich feathers attract dust. I found one for $4.99 at a department store.)

When cleaning, remember to always work from top to bottom. Dirt follows gravity. You don't want to clean a counter and then dust a cupboard above the counter, scattering dirt onto your newly cleaned surface.

Walk the perimeter of your house. As you confront every surface before you, whip out what is necessary to spit shine the surface or object before you, continuously working from top to bottom.

Spray and wipe the mirror. Polish the wood. Scrape the pie dough off the counter with your plastic scraper or use the toothbrush to de-grime the water spigot. Scour the sink. Dust your mantel objects with the feather duster. Then, whack the duster on your ankle so the dust falls into the carpet. You will vacuum it up later.

As for your bathroom, store some specific supplies there. This is an exception to the tools-in-the-apron rule. Store products needed for the toilet in the individual bathrooms. (Be sure to keep them out of the reach of children.)

Clean the bathroom working from top to bottom. After cleaning the surfaces, make one more sweep around the house to vacuum and damp mop.

In no time your abode will be ready for company. Now, grab your gear and begin!

When you get your weekly cleaning routine down pat—and can perform it quickly—it will free up more time for others. Think through the points in this next section to come up with your own quickstep cleaning routine.

MY QUICKSTEP CLEANING STRATEGY

The aspect of cleaning the house that most frustrates me is

_____

Quickstep cleaning might help me clear this hurdle by

_____

Below is a list of the tools needed. Put a check mark by those you already have.

- Apron
- Glass cleaner
- All-purpose cleaner
- Toilet-bowl cleaner
- Rags
- Sponge

- Wood polish
- Scouring powder
- Toothbrush
- Plastic scraper
- Ostrich feather duster

Now look at the list again and circle any tools you need to purchase. Be sure to add them to your regular shopping list.

I will take a stab at speed cleaning my home. The date I will try this is

_____ .

day 10
Sharing Some Secret Family Recipes

erhaps some of our family's favorite dishes will become yours as well. Here is a sampling of some of the standby ones I make for family and serve often to our guests.

Whole-Grain Oat Waffles

This original recipe was given to me over twenty years ago by my college best friend, Kelly. Whip up the batter, pour some in the waffle maker, and watch them disappear! For the deluxe version, we top them with butter, peanut butter, homemade raspberry jam, and pure maple syrup.

Ingredients

3 cups	quick oats (not old-fashioned oats)
1 cup	whole wheat pastry flour (may use unbleached all-purpose flour but do not use regular whole wheat flour)

2 teaspoons	baking soda
1 teaspoon	sugar
1 teaspoon	salt
¼ cup	butter, melted and slightly cooled (½ stick)
4 cups	full-fat buttermilk (not low-fat)
4	eggs, beaten
	Cooking spray

Directions

In a large bowl, mix oats, flour, baking soda, sugar, and salt. In a medium-sized bowl, slowly whisk melted butter into the buttermilk. Add beaten eggs and whisk again. Blend in dry ingredients just until well blended. Let batter rest 5 minutes.

Following the directions for your waffle maker as to whether you need to use cooking spray or not and the amount of batter to use, pour batter into waffle maker. Bake according to waffle maker directions. (I bake them 2 minutes and then flip and bake 1½ minutes more.) Serve immediately. Makes six round seven-inch-diameter waffles.

Wild Rice Chicken

This dish looks oh-so-fancy, but it's actually extremely simple to make. Best of all, the main dish and side dish are baked in one pan. Add a veggie salad, bread, and a dessert, and dinner is done! Perfect for company.

Ingredients

2 cups	chicken stock (or canned chicken broth)
½ cup	Italian dressing made with olive oil
16 ounces	petite diced canned tomatoes, with juice

¼ cup	finely chopped green pepper
½ cup	finely chopped yellow onion
½ cup	finely chopped carrots
¾ teaspoon	dried basil
½ teaspoon	garlic powder
¼ teaspoon	black pepper
½ teaspoon	salt
6-ounce box	long grain and wild rice (I use Uncle Ben's)
4	boneless, skinless chicken breasts
	Fresh Parmesan cheese

Directions

Preheat oven to 350 degrees. In a large saucepan, combine chicken stock, Italian dressing, tomatoes, peppers, onion, carrots, basil, garlic powder, pepper, salt, and the spice packet in the box of rice. Cover and bring to a rolling boil. Reduce heat and simmer, covered, for 5 minutes. Remove from heat and add rice, stirring well.

Coat a 9 x 13 x 2-inch pan with cooking spray and carefully pour the rice mixture into the pan, spreading evenly. Place the chicken breasts on top of the rice and cover pan with foil, sealing tightly. Bake for 1 hour and 10 minutes at 350 degrees. To serve, spoon some of the rice mixture, along with one chicken breast, onto in-dividual plates. Top the chicken breast with fresh grated Parmesan cheese. Serves four.

Roasted Brussels Sprouts with Cranberries and Pine Nuts

One of my all-time picks for a late-summer or fall "company is coming!" meal. The unique union of brussels sprouts, cranberries, and pine nuts makes this dish unforgettable. May be made in a cookie sheet with sides but is best prepared in a cast-iron pan to crisp them perfectly.

Ingredients

1 pound fresh	brussels sprouts
¼ cup	olive oil
1½ teaspoons	fresh, minced garlic
	Salt and pepper to taste
3 tablespoons	pure maple syrup
⅓ cup	dried cranberries
⅓ cup	pine nuts

Directions

Heat oven to 400 degrees. Trim off bottoms of brussels sprouts and slice each in half from top to bottom. In a large bowl, toss sprouts in the oil and garlic.

Lightly grease the bottom of a large cast-iron pan and place sprouts, cut side down, in the pan in a single layer. Sprinkle with salt and pepper to taste and lightly drizzle with maple syrup.

On the middle rack of the oven, roast until brown and tender, about 25–30 minutes for medium-sized brussels sprouts. You may need to adjust the time up or down if they are small or jumbo. You want them to be slightly browned, but not burnt.

Remove pan and sprinkle on cranberries and pine nuts. Turn oven on broil. Return to oven and broil 1–2 minutes, watching carefully so they brown slightly but do not burn. Serve immediately. Serves 4.

Oatmeal Dinner Rolls

These are a snap to make and are delicious warm from the oven. Serve with cinnamon honey butter (recipe below).

Ingredients

2 cups	water
1 cup	quick oats
3 tablespoons	butter
1 tablespoon	yeast (1 packet)
⅓ cup	very warm water (between 105 and 110 degrees)
1 tablespoon	sugar
⅓ cup	brown sugar
1½ teaspoons	salt
4¾–5¼ cups	bread flour

Directions

In a medium-sized saucepan over medium-high heat, boil the 2 cups water, oats, and butter for 1 minute. Set aside.

In a large bowl, thoroughly mix yeast, ⅓ cup warm water, and sugar. Let stand for 3–5 minutes, then add brown sugar and salt.

Add oat mixture and mix well. Then add in flour, just enough to make a slightly (but not overly) stiff dough. Turn into a lightly oiled large bowl. Cover the bowl with a clean kitchen towel and let rise until doubled, about 1–1½ hours.

Punch down and separate into three balls of dough. Then separate each of those into halves. Take each half and separate into three equal pieces. The result should be 18 equal pieces. Roll each into a ball. Place nine rolls each in two greased round cake pans. Do so by placing one in the center and then place eight more equidistant around the center. Cover with plastic wrap that has been sprayed with cooking spray to avoid sticking. Let rise 20–30 minutes, until sides of rolls begin to touch. While rising, preheat oven to 350 degrees.

Remove plastic wrap. Bake at 350 degrees for 20–25 minutes. Do not over-brown. (Rolls can be covered with a piece of foil laid on top but not sealed to prevent them from browning too much.) Remove and cool. Store any leftovers covered, at room temperature. Yield: 18 rolls.

Cinnamon Honey Butter

Butter gets a kiss of some warm spice and a smack of sweet. Heavenly!

Ingredients

1 pound (4 sticks) real butter
½ cup honey
¾ teaspoon ground cinnamon

Directions

While still cold, cut butter in chunks and place in a bowl. Allow to soften to room temperature. Using an electric mixer on low speed, blend in the honey until well incorporated. Sprinkle on cinnamon and blend again.

Place the softened butter in a few small decorative bowls and cover with plastic wrap. You may also spread some of the softened butter onto parchment paper and shape into a log. Roll the log up so it is well covered with the parchment paper and then, using twist ties, seal up each end.

To really take it up a notch, you may also spread the softened butter in candy molds to make individual servings for a fancier presentation. Store in the refrigerator until ready to serve. Before serving, allowed to sit out at room temperature for 15 to 30 minutes to soften slightly.

FIND ME Somebody TO LOVE

day 11

Tell Me, What Do You Have?

The book of 2 Kings introduces us to two diverse women. One is a destitute widow, uncertain whether she will be able to feed her family. The second woman is rich, married, and childless. However, both women have this in common: As their circumstances turn dismal, and the well-being of someone they love is in peril, it is then that God moves, using the prophet Elisha to help meet their needs and calm their souls.

While we might think of Old Testament prophets as being single men who roamed about proclaiming the Word of the Lord or who lived a monastic and reclusive existence, this was not the case. Although they performed a sacred service by their occupation, they weren't forbidden from marrying or becoming fathers. They lived normal lives in homes with their families, enduring life's ups and downs like the rest of us.

The first woman we meet was once married to such a prophet. Second Kings 4:1 lists him as a servant of Elisha and a man who revered the Lord. However, when he died, his widow found herself not only grieving but

also fearful that her children would be taken from her as well and forced
into slavery to pay a debt.

She presented her dilemma to the prophet Elisha to see what he would
say. "Elisha asked her, 'What can I do for you? Tell me, what do you have
in the house?' She said, 'Your servant has nothing in the house except a
jar of oil'" (2 Kings 4:2 NIV).

Upon hearing she had only a small jar of oil, Elisha set about to work
with what she had. Soon she found herself canvassing the neighborhood,
asking for empty jars. Then she and her sons began to fill the jars with
their meager amount of oil. Miraculously, the oil flowed until all the jars
were filled.

Elisha then instructed her to sell the oil. Apparently, the oil had mul-
tiplied so profusely that the proceeds would settle her debt and offer a
living for herself and her offspring.

Immediately after the account of this woman, we see Elisha interacting
with a Shunammite wife. Ordinarily, females were introduced with regard
to their husband's position or financial status. However, this Shunammite
is described as a "well-to-do woman," indicating she was a woman of
affluence before getting hitched. She bids the prophet to join her family
for a meal. This gesture sets in motion a practice of him staying with
them—in a special room just for this purpose—whenever he comes to
town. What a fabulous example of hospitality!

Elisha longs to repay her for her kindness, so he speaks to her through
his servant Gehazi. He asks the woman what Elisha could do for her—
perhaps speak on her behalf to the king or commander of the army.
But this woman doesn't want notoriety or a political favor. She wants a
bouncing baby boy.

Elisha's discovery of her heart's desire sets off a chain of events. He declares that she will become pregnant. Though she doesn't believe him, within a year she gives birth and is already deciding what she'll dress the new darling in for his very first Instagram shot.

However, one day her joy turns to sorrow as her son experiences immense pain in his head that results in his death. She then places the child on Elisha's bed and hurries toward Mount Carmel, traveling the fifteen-plus miles as fast as she can. When Elisha hears of the tragic situation, he speeds to the boy, and then God, through Elisha's actions, raises the child back to life.

Although the life circumstances of these women were different, there is one thing they have in common. In each instance, God brought about a miracle based on this notion: "Tell me, what do you have?" In the case of the widow, she had olive oil. In the case of the Shunammite woman, she had faith. Yet each of these women needed to go fetch what it was that was needed for their miracles to transpire. The widow needed to fetch the oil. The Shunammite woman needed to fetch the prophet.

For both, it was something they already possessed. When they sprang into action, taking what they already had and offering it to God, he brought about the miraculous resolution to their troubling dilemmas.

What about you? Do you think it will take a miracle for you to ever get the hang of this hospitality lifestyle? Or, did you once upon a time have a passion for reaching out to others that fizzled, and now it needs to be brought back to life?

Gather your resources and fetch your faith. Expect God to act, and don't be surprised if he uses one or more of his people in the process. God is best positioned to act when we take what we have, tuck it in an envelope of trust, and offer it back to him—our Provider and the Author and Perfecter of our faith (Hebrews 12:2).

Second Peter 1:3 states, "His divine power has given us everything required for life and godliness through the knowledge of him who called us by his own glory and goodness."

God has already given us everything required for life—and for a life of godliness.

So tell me, what do *you* have? A home—even if it is a small apartment? Food in your fridge, even if it seems basic rather than gourmet? An oven that could crank out a batch of muffins or cookies to deliver to someone, along with some cheer—even if that oven hasn't been cleaned in months? A car that could be used to transport someone out for coffee or lunch—even if it isn't a newer model or ever so slightly fancy?

Yes, tell me, what do you have?

The Lord can take what you already have and use it to be the answer to someone's prayers. Don't despise the small things. Decide now that you will use whatever resources God has given you to reach others for his glory.

Below, scrawl out a one-sentence prayer for the week, asking God to enable you to use what you already have to minister to others.

My ONE-SENTENCE PRAYER
FOR THE WEEK

_____

_____

_____

_____

_____

_____

_____

_____

day 12

Won't You Be My Neighbor?

When my husband was a youth pastor, I was sometimes in charge of the games for youth group. We often played one of the crowd favorites. It was called "Do you love your neighbor?" Here is the gist of it:

All the members of the youth group stood in a circle with one person standing alone in the middle. That person would walk up to someone and ask them the question, "Do you love your neighbor?" If the person they asked said yes, everyone moved one place to their right while the person in the middle of the circle tried to jump in and grab a spot, leaving someone else stuck in the middle. However, if the person being asked the question answered no, they were then asked a follow-up question, "Well then, what kind of neighbors *do* you like?"

Then, the game got a little creative.

The person being asked the question would describe the variety of neighbor that they did like. They might assert that they enjoyed neighbors with blue eyes. Or they were currently wearing red tennis shoes. At that point, everyone in the circle who fit the description given had to switch places with someone else. It became a frenzy of movement as everyone tried to trade spots.

While that was happening, the question-asker tried to jump in and grab a spot. If they were successful, then a new person was now left in the middle of the circle. They became the next one to ask the important question, "Do you love your neighbor?"

Ever the maximizing youth leaders, of course my husband and I had to sneak in a little lesson on loving your actual neighbor once the game was over, using the biblical account of the man who garnered the moniker "The Good Samaritan."

This story is so renowned it has attained proverbial status. For example, municipalities enact Good Samaritan laws that offer legal protection to anyone who tries to assist someone in peril, should their well-intended efforts go awry.

You'd think since the story of the Good Samaritan is a classic one, known even to those outside the church, this would not need to be a lesson we'd have to preach to others—and often to ourselves—over and over again. But it is.

Here's a little refresher of this story, found in Luke 10:25–37. It was all prompted by a question from a lawyer:

> Then an expert in the law stood up to test him, saying, "Teacher, what must I do to inherit eternal life?"
>
> Luke 10:25

Jesus asked him what was written in the law, and the man responded:

> "Love the Lord your God with all your heart, with all your soul, with all your strength, and with all your mind," and "your neighbor as yourself."
>
> Luke 10:27

Probing a little further, the lawyer queried Jesus, "Who is my neighbor?" It was then that Jesus launched into the famous parable. He spoke of a man going down from Jerusalem to Jericho. Muggers attacked him, took his belongings, and even stole the garments off his back. They also beat him, leaving him half dead.

A priest meandered by. Surely a religious man would help this victim, right? Nope. He passed by him, keeping his distance by walking on the other side of the road. A Levite—one who performed sacred tasks in the temple—also happened along. Perchance he would see the sacred task before him of helping a wounded soul. Not even a chance.

It took a Samaritan, from a race hated by the Jews, to notice the battered man and have compassion on him. He drizzled oil and wine on his wounds, bound them up, then acted as an ancient Uber by placing him on his own animal and taking him to a local Airbnb. He went so far as to Venmo the innkeeper some cash to care for the victim's expenses. (Okay, maybe I've described it a bit differently than Luke did, but you get the picture!)

Jesus questioned the lawyer, inquiring which of the three people had behaved as a neighbor. The lawyer responded that the man who displayed mercy was a neighbor. Then Jesus instructed him to go and do the same.

Now, not many of us are going to happen upon somebody who has just been roughed up by a gang of thugs. However, there is an important lesson for us in this timeless story: We limit ourselves when we only interact with—and care for—the people within our inner circle of friends and family. God's family is much bigger. There are so many other souls whose lives we could better if only we expanded our concept of just who our neighbors are.

In our current culture—severely steeped in social media—we decide whom we will "like," "follow," or let view our posts. We create exclusive groups on Facebook. We often exclude, rather than expand. But God's Word calls us to reach beyond our default and attempt to connect with all sorts of souls.

Galatians 6:10 (NIV) urges, "Therefore, as we have opportunity, let us do good to all people, especially to those who belong to the family of believers." Guess what *all* means in the original text? Yep. All means all! It can be translated as *of every kind* and *the whole*. I love the concept that conjures up in my mind. When we include all—people of every kind—we come together to make a whole.

May you go about your day today being on the lookout for new neighbors.

Let's broaden our view of just who are "our people." Work through the following questions, designed to help you both notice and reach out to those whom God has put in your path.

Ponder AND Pray

Think about a typical weekday for you—from the time you get up until the time you go to bed. Write down all the people you see face-to-face in the course of the day. You don't have to use specific names; general categories will work just fine, such as "co-workers in my office" or "the other parents on the sidelines of the soccer field." Scroll through them in your mind and write them down below.

_____

_____

_____

_____

Look back over that list. Circle any people or categories you have made an effort to get to know. Viewing those who are left, place a star beside the one you might feel God prompting you to reach out to. Now, what small gesture could you do this week to show that person some love? Write your thoughts in the space below.

_____

_____

_____

_____

Whip out your phone and open its calendar app, or grab your paper calendar, if that is how you roll. Give yourself a deadline by which you will follow through on your good intention to show them love with a thoughtful gesture.

Memory Verse 3

For the whole law is fulfilled in one statement:
Love your *neighbor* as yourself.

GALATIANS 5:14

day 13

Just Open Your Eyes
(and Ears!)

$\mathcal{I}$ once knew a college instructor who gave a unique at-home assignment. Her students were required to wear military-grade
earplugs and black blindfolds for an entire eight-hour period
one day at home, trying their best to make it through the day without
seeing anything or hearing much. It was so eye-opening! (Yes, pun totally
intended.)

At first, students thought the assignment was novel, maybe even a little
fun. But after an hour or more passed, they grew very frustrated. It was
so difficult to navigate without using their sight. And since all the sounds
were very muffled, listening to others' words was not much help either.
Students bumped their knees on coffee tables. They pulled the wrong
items out of the refrigerator. And then what a fiasco it was when they tried
to make themselves some lunch! When the eight-hour period was over,

and the blindfolds came off and the earplugs were removed, what relief they felt. It was a whole new world when they could see and hear again.

While this clever assignment was designed to spark empathy in these students for the blind and deaf, I can't help but think about how often we are spiritually lacking when it comes to really seeing and hearing the people in our lives, walking by them because we are either oblivious or purposefully trying to avoid them. Many souls materialize before our eyes and ears each day—whether in person or on a screen we are holding—but so often we simply do not see. We do not hear. Or maybe we do *hear*, but we don't *listen*.

If only we would intentionally tune our ears and focus our eyes, we would discover a whole new world. We might stop missing so many of the opportunities right before us.

Living this way starts by being on the lookout for what is known around my house as a "heart-drop." A heart-drop is when a person, either directly or in a cryptic way, gives you a peek into their heart. It may be through actual words, or you may pick up on a feeling, perhaps sadness or loneliness. It could even be a simple preference or "like" of theirs, such as their most-loved snack or a favorite sports team. Or maybe you sense anxiousness or worry in their voice when they mention an upcoming doctor's appointment. It is a matter of listening between the lines.

When we hear a heart-drop, we can brush it aside and go on our busy way. Or, we can respond with an act of kindness. It may be words of reassurance, a clever small gift, an act of service, or the gift of your time.

The concept of heart-drops has caused me to become a better listener and has provided me with numerous opportunities to show love to the members of my family, to acquaintances, and even to complete strangers.

Hearing—and then responding to—a heart-drop is an art we can cultivate. It can lead to the most wonderful times of encouragement as we make it our habit to listen, look, and love.

Let's focus today on really looking and listening, noticing those in our lives who least expect to be seen but who could greatly benefit from a kind word, loving gesture, or helpful action we could perform.

Ponder AND Pray

Time to focus on looking and listening. What—and more importantly whom—have we been missing as we go about our daily routines? Take a few moments to work through the following questions, designed to help you discover the ministry opportunities all around you.

Loving our neighbors requires us to be attentive to their needs. How attentive are you? During a typical day, are you taking note of others and their feelings, or are you focused on your own life and rather oblivious to those you encounter? Place an X on the continuum below, showing where you stand.

Pretty Oblivious	Rarely Attentive	Average	Somewhat Attentive	Totally Tuned In

How'd ya do? Do you desire to move that X, becoming a more observant neighbor? What do you need to change to make this happen?

_____

_____

_____

_____

_____

_____

TAKE ROOT *and* TAKE ACTION

Do you recall our optional memory verse for this section: "For the whole law is fulfilled in one statement: Love your neighbor as yourself" (Galatians 5:14)? We are so great at loving ourselves, aren't we? We make sure we are fed and clothed, and that we keep warm during the cold months and cool during the sweltering season. Have you ever really thought of the concept of loving your neighbor as yourself? It was a somewhat vague concept to me until somebody challenged me to think of all the ways I make sure that I am cared for and comfortable.

They then said I should seek to make sure that others in my life, especially those on the fringe, are cared for in this same way.

Time to allow this verse from Galatians to take root and take action. Choose one way you care for yourself and then schedule a time to care for someone else in this same way.

One example might be that you make sure you have proper hygiene practices. In fact, you love flowery-smelling bubble baths or fruity-scented lotions. Could you scour your community for a shelter for homeless or battered women that is in need of hygiene products for residents? Purchase some and deliver them in person, meeting some of the residents if you are allowed.

Don't just let the words of Galatians 5:14 stay printed only in your Bible. Give them wings, springing them into action. Write below how you will love and care for someone else in a way you already love and care for yourself. Then, follow through and do it!

day 14
Don't Fail to Prepare

ypically, I try to avoid clichés like the plague. (Ha! Except I didn't in that sentence!) An old cliché you may have heard is this: If you fail to plan, you are planning to fail. Though it might sound tired and typical to our ears, it is true nonetheless. And this includes when it comes to opening our homes—as well as our very lives—to others. We must be prepared.

With a little forethought and a little bit more action, we can set ourselves up for success when it comes to hospitality. This concept isn't limited to the space inside our homes. We can prepare our vehicles and even our office desks to aid in our quest to show a little kindness to those in our lives.

First, let's start with our homes. We can prepare for company, even the unexpected variety, long before they knock on our doors. Here are a few strategies for making your house guest-friendly.

- Be sure to have extra sets of sheets and towels clean and folded in whatever room will house your guests. This way there won't be any last-minute scrambling should overnight company come calling.

- When you are traveling and staying at a hotel or bed-and-breakfast that provides you with trial-sized bottles of shampoo, conditioner, and body wash, take home what you don't use. You can add these to a small welcome basket for your guests when they arrive.

- Another item to add to a welcome basket is a handful of chocolates. But rather than having to dash off to the store, plan ahead to always have some of these sweet treats on hand. After major holidays, many stores mark down foil-wrapped seasonal chocolates, sometimes up to 90 percent off. Often, they are wrapped in such a manner that they are not holiday specific. Also, many of them do not become out of date for up to one year. Grab a bag or two that are wrapped in a generic way, perhaps in gold, silver, or red foil. Stash them away so you can use some to round out a welcome basket.

- Consider getting a small single-serve coffeemaker or electric teapot for your guest room, if you have one. Place some tea bags and single-serve cups in a basket to complete their personal coffee bar.

- Watch for sales on large, fluffy, one-size-fits-most cotton robes. Having one of these on hand for overnight guests makes them feel pampered. And it is not typically an item someone packs to take with them on a trip since it is so bulky and would take up a lot of room in their suitcase.

- Other items to be on the lookout for to add to a welcome basket: granola bars, single-use beauty face masks, disposable razors, cotton swabs, trial-sized bottles of mouthwash or tubes of toothpaste, and colorful washcloths that you can roll up and tie with a lace ribbon.

Next, think through your vehicle—yes, your car. With a little preparation you can have it be a place of hospitality as well. Here are some helpful trinkets and treats to stash in an automobile:

- Store a tote bag in your car that includes some items that might be needed should you—and others—find yourselves waiting, perhaps at a sporting event that is delayed due to weather. In this bag, place some protein or whole-grain fruit bars, small bottles of water, bags of nuts or dried fruits, and a couple of crossword puzzles or brainteaser books, along with a few pens. Sure, you could sit and play on your phones, but if preserving the phones' batteries is a concern, you will still have something to do to pass the time.

- Fill another small bag with some first-aid items such as bandages, triple antibiotic cream, sunscreen, and insect repellent.

- Consider having a small box in the back of your vehicle that contains items to help children pass the time, such as sturdy kids' books, a jump rope, a Frisbee, or a few rubber balls.

- Sometimes when we are driving around town in our vehicles, we may encounter individuals who are homeless, often standing on a street corner, holding cardboard signs. Put together a few individual bags that you can hand out to these people when you see them. In them include some protein-packed snacks such as nuts or meal-replacement bars, a gift card to a local eatery that is within walking distance, a trial-sized package of tissues, some personal hygiene wet wipes, and some confections that will not melt, such as hard mints, or fruit-flavored or butterscotch candies. You may even want to tuck in a booklet of the Gospel of

John for some reading material along with a tract that tells the Gospel story and explains the process of salvation.

Next, we have your office desk. Be ready in a blink to scatter a little kindness by having these items on hand:

- A small basket on your desk that will serve as a perpetual stream of treats for any of your co-workers who want to grab one. Again, look for after-season sales or clearance bins at the store to purchase individual bags of trail mix, nuts, dried fruits, salty snacks, or candies.
- If allowed, have your office or cubicle smelling sweet with a plug-in warmer of essential oils.
- Make sure your co-workers know you care about them and are willing to pray for them, should they desire you to. To facilitate this happening, have either a small basket or decorative box with a lid. Near it, place some sticky notes or note cards and a pen. Co-workers may write their prayer request and place it in the basket or box. Again, only do this if your place of employment allows you to.

And finally, think about that purse. When her kids were all younger, my mother-in-law was known for not only having a large purse but for having it stocked full of goodies and helpful items. Again, think non-melting treats, first-aid items, or things that may help in a pinch, such as a sewing kit or stain-remover stick.

If you just take a little time to prepare ahead, you can be welcoming wherever you are!

day 15

A Freezer Full of Love

ith these freezer recipes, you will easily have a meal in minutes for your drop-in company, whether for breakfast, lunch, or dinner, or just a tasty snack.

Quiche in a Bag

Don't just think breakfast when it comes to this mouthwatering quiche. It works just as well for a light lunch or supper.

Ingredients

2 cups	cooked, crumbled turkey sausage (or cooked, diced ham)
½ cup	raw, diced red or green pepper
½ cup	canned mushrooms, drained
½ cup	minced onion
2 cups	shredded sharp cheddar cheese

4 cups	whole milk
8	large eggs
½ teaspoon	hot sauce
1 cup	unbleached flour
1 tablespoon	baking powder

Optional: Two deep-dish frozen pie crusts (may also use refrigerated, roll-out crusts)

Directions

Combine meat, peppers, mushrooms, onion, and cheese in a large bowl. In another large bowl, mix the milk, eggs, hot sauce, flour, and baking powder on low speed until well blended. Pour into the meat mixture. Divide the liquid quiche into two gallon-sized freezer bags and seal tightly, squeezing out as much air as possible. Freeze.

To prepare, thaw overnight in the fridge. Shake the bag to incorporate ingredients. For a crustless version, pour into a pie pan that has been coated with cooking spray. (You may also pour it into a ready-made crust such as a deep-dish frozen one or a refrigerated, roll-out variety.) Bake at 350 degrees for 40–45 minutes, until a knife inserted in the center comes out clean. Cool 10 minutes and serve. Each quiche serves 8.

Farmers Market Muffins

Hands-down my favorite make-ahead muffin to have stashed in the freezer. The vibrant colors of the fruits and veggies make it so appealing. And just wait until you see how moist they turn out!

Ingredients

2 cups	all-purpose flour
1¼ cups	white sugar
2 teaspoons	baking soda
1½ teaspoons	ground cinnamon
½ teaspoon	ground nutmeg
⅓ teaspoon	salt
1 cup	shredded carrots
1 cup	shredded zucchini
½ cup	raisins
⅔ cup	chopped walnuts
½ cup	flaked coconut
1	medium-sized baking apple, peeled, cored, and shredded (Granny Smith, Golden Delicious, Fuji, or Cortland are great varieties.)
3	large eggs
1 cup	olive oil
1½ teaspoons	vanilla extract

Directions

Preheat oven to 350 degrees. Line a 12-muffin tin with paper muffin liners or spray with cooking spray with flour, designed for baking.

In a large bowl, mix together flour, sugar, baking soda, cinnamon, nutmeg, and salt. Blend in the carrots, zucchini, raisins, nuts, coconut, and apple just until combined.

In a separate medium-sized bowl, beat together eggs, oil, and vanilla. Stir egg mixture into the flour mixture, just until moistened. Spoon batter into prepared muffin cups.

Bake in preheated oven for 18–20 minutes, until a toothpick inserted into center of a muffin comes out clean. Cool completely and freeze in freezer bags, pressing out as much air as you can when sealing the bags. Store in freezer for up to two months. Thaw before serving. Makes 12 muffins.

Italial Stuffed Shells

Your guests will never suspect that this tasty Italian dish was pulled out of your deep freeze. Don't worry. Your secret is safe with me! This recipe makes enough to cook half of it now and freeze the other half for another day.

Ingredients

36–40	jumbo pasta shells (12-ounce box)
32 ounces	small curd cottage cheese
24 ounces	shredded Italian blend or mozzarella cheese
¾ cup	fresh shredded Parmesan cheese
4	eggs
1 teaspoon	dried oregano
¾ teaspoon	dried basil
½ teaspoon	dried garlic
½ teaspoon	salt
¼ teaspoon	pepper

Have on hand on cooking day:

Two 31-ounce jars	spaghetti sauce
	Fresh Parmesan cheese for grating

Directions

In a large pot of boiling water, cook the shells half the recommended time. Drain and cool slightly. Combine cottage, Italian, and Parmesan cheeses, eggs, oregano, basil, garlic, salt, and pepper. Place cheese mixture in a gallon plastic bag with a zip closure. Snip off one corner of the bag and pipe the cheese mixture equally into the shells. There is plenty of cheese mixture, so stuff them generously. Place shells on a cookie sheet lined with wax paper and freeze for four hours. Transfer to two two-gallon plastic freezer bags, squeezing as much air out as you can when closing. Freeze bags.

To prepare one bag, spray a 9 x 13-inch pan with cooking spray and spread ½ cup of spaghetti sauce from one jar over the bottom of the pan. Arrange shells from freezer bag in the pan and spread the remainder of the jar of sauce over the shells, covering well. Cover with foil and bake for 60 minutes at 350 degrees. Remove foil and bake 10–15 minutes more until heated through. Garnish with freshly grated Parmesan cheese. Each bag, made with one jar of sauce, serves six.

Chocolate Peanut Butter Bars

The classic pairing of chocolate and peanut butter is kicked up a notch with this freezer treat. Bet your guests can't eat just one!

Ingredients

½ cup	salted butter
1 cup	graham cracker crumbs
2 cups	powdered sugar
1⅛ cups	creamy peanut butter, divided
1 cup	semisweet chocolate chips

Directions

Using parchment paper or foil, line an 8 x 8-inch square baking pan. Melt butter in a saucepan over very low heat or in the microwave. In a large bowl combine the melted butter, graham cracker crumbs, and powdered sugar until well blended. Stir in 1 cup of peanut butter and press into lined baking pan.

In a medium-sized saucepan over very low heat, melt remaining 2 tablespoons of peanut butter with the chocolate chips, stirring with a whisk until well blended. Use a rubber spatula to spread mixture over the peanut butter layer. Allow to cool in the refrigerator, uncovered, for 1 hour or until set.

Cut into squares. Place in freezer containers between sheets of parchment paper. Thaw about 20 minutes at room temperature before serving. Makes 16 two-inch squares.

DISCOVERING YOUR *Niche*

day 16
Our Need to Nurture

*A*n American psychologist named Harry Harlow grew curious about the subject of love and nurture and a human's innate need for them. In a few provocative experimentations conducted during the 1960s, he set out to find any conclusions he might reach about the effects of love, specifically on the absence of love in a newborn.

Perhaps you remember learning in school about his study using young rhesus monkeys. He set up for each monkey two surrogate "moms." One was a sterile and cold wire fake mother monkey that provided food through a baby bottle secured to the wire. The second mom was a cuddly, cloth replica monkey that did not give food but offered warmth and a sense of security.

He removed baby monkeys from their natural mothers a few hours after birth, a controversial move that was considered cruel by many, even in his own profession. He then placed them with their two fake mothers to be raised. When this occurred, the infant primates spent drastically less time with their wire mothers than with their cloth mothers. They latched on to the wire mothers only when their hunger drove them to eat. The rest of the time they clung to their cuddly, soft moms for security and comfort.

Any of us human beings who have been on the earth long enough to reach adulthood wouldn't argue that we all have a need to feel loved, nurtured, and secure. But there is a corresponding need that sometimes we don't think about. That is the need not only to receive, but also to give love.

Professor Raj Raghunathan, PhD, made this observation in a piece he wrote for *Psychology Today*:

> In our pursuit of the need to be loved, however, most of us fail to recognize that we have a parallel need: *the need to love and care for others*. This desire, it turns out, is just as strong as the need to be loved and nurtured.[1]

How often have you thought of this need for nurturing others? We might observe this in tiny children as they cuddle a teddy bear or doll, or perhaps lovingly hold a soft puppy or even their newborn younger sibling for the first time. But as we grow older and are immersed in our self-centered culture, nurturing others becomes easy to dismiss. We grow far more adept at looking out for ourselves—making sure we are fed, clothed, comfortable, and secure—than seeking to provide those things for others.

The concept of our possessing a need to nurture isn't just a notion we find in modern-day psychology. We find snapshots of it on the pages of Scripture. Sure, we need comfort. But it is not an end in itself. It has a purpose in the family of God. It even has a progression.

First, it is God who comforts us. Just look at a few of the places in Scripture where we see the comfort, love, compassion, and care of our heavenly Father:

Psalm 23:4: Even when I go through the darkest valley, I fear no danger, for you are with me; your rod and your staff—they comfort me.

Psalm 119:49–50: Remember your word to your servant; you have given me hope through it. This is my comfort in my affliction: Your promise has given me life.

Isaiah 49:13: Shout for joy, you heavens! Earth, rejoice! Mountains break into joyful shouts! For the Lord has comforted his people, and will have compassion on his afflicted ones.

Isaiah 51:12: I—I am the one who comforts you. Who are you that you should fear humans who die, or a son of man who is given up like grass?

And, lest we think his love for us will someday run out, the most beautiful verse about this of all . . .

Lamentations 3:22–23: Because of the Lord's faithful love we do not perish, for his mercies never end. They are new every morning; great is your faithfulness!

New every single morning! The God of compassion, comfort, and mercy never tires of caring for his children.

But is all this lavish love just for us to nestle ourselves in and feel safe? Or is there another point to it all?

Second Corinthians 1:3–4 (NIV) gives us the complete picture: "Praise be to the God and Father of our Lord Jesus Christ, the Father of compassion and the God of all comfort, who comforts us in all our troubles, so that we can comfort those in any trouble with the comfort we ourselves receive from God."

Comforting others is part of our marching orders as Christians here on earth. But God doesn't just send us off on our own to somehow figure out how to do it. He equips us first by providing comfort for us whenever we face troubles. Then, armed with the strength we have received during our times of turmoil, we can effectively comfort others with what we have received from God. This string of comfort is the thread God uses to knit our hearts to others as we not only receive love and comfort when we need it, but we openhandedly give it to others as well.

There is such a need for comfort because we live in a fallen world—full of heartache, disappointments, sickness, and sorrow, not to mention evil. We have trouble of all kinds surrounding us on every side. Sometimes, I admit, this fact surprises me. But then I think of Jesus' words in John 16:33 (NIV):

I have told you these things, so that in me you may have peace. In this world you will have trouble. But take heart! I have overcome the world.

Jesus said that in the world we will have trouble. Not *might* have trouble—*will*. Why then, I wonder, does it seem to surprise me when it appears in my life or the life of another?

However, armed with the fact that Jesus has overcome the world, clasped to the comfort we ourselves have received from God, we can take our place in God's ministry of comfort and help to lighten a load, cheer a weary soul, or encourage the downcast.

This isn't a onetime assignment. In 1 Thessalonians 4:9–10, the apostle Paul stated,

> About brotherly love: You don't need me to write you because you your-selves are taught by God to love one another. In fact, you are doing this toward all the brothers and sisters in the entire region of Macedonia. But we encourage you, brothers and sisters, to do this even more.

Let's make this our constant chorus: We will love, nurture, and com-fort. And then? *We will do this even more.*

There are souls in your life who need your nurture. Let's set out to find them and complete the circle of comfort that began when God first comforted you.

Below, write out a one-sentence prayer for the week, asking God to kindle in you a desire to nurture and comfort others, armed with the comfort you have already received from him.

My
ONE-SENTENCE PRAYER
FOR THE WEEK

_____

_____

_____

_____

_____

_____

_____

_____

day 17

On Puzzle Pieces
and Purpose

o you make New Year's resolutions? Or if that is not your jam, maybe you choose a single word for the year like *brave* or *serve*. Or perhaps you, like many believers, have a particular Scripture you refer to as your life verse, such as the ever-popular Jeremiah 29:11: "'For I know the plans I have for you'—this is the LORD's declaration—'plans for your well-being, not for disaster, to give you a future and a hope.'"

Making resolutions, selecting a word, or picking out a passage of Scripture are all marvelous gestures. They can help us to focus on a goal or maintain a perspective that keeps our thoughts centered on God's kingdom. But let's dig even deeper than that. Rather than just coming up with a temporary word or a list of goals that will carry us through the next twelve months, let's seek to find our overall purpose—where we fit in the plans God has for the people in our lives and especially in our churches.

When I was a young Christian, I closely watched some women who had been believers much longer than I as they served in the church or played important roles in the lives of their friends, family members, co-workers, or neighbors. I was still in college, just trying to figure out my next step, wondering what my future held as far as employment, marriage, and beyond. But as I spent time with these women of faith, I attentively studied them. They seemed to have such purpose when it came to the local body of believers to which they belonged, connected by serving in a myriad of ways.

They baked cookies for the church nursery or concocted a delicious casserole when there was a death in the congregation. They allowed the youth group to meet in their backyard, playing crazy games and devouring buckets full of taco salad. Sometimes on a weeknight, their living rooms might transform into a retreat for the women's Bible study group of about a dozen. They put the coffeepot on, dragged some chairs in from the dining room, and provided a welcoming and safe haven, where together these Christians could study God's Word and pray for each other, sharing whatever was on their heavy hearts. And one of them actually taught the women's group, studying thick commentaries and cracking open a volume of Hebrew and Greek words and their meanings to try to teach the Word of God with the utmost of care.

When they saw a need they could meet, they met it. They weren't church workaholics, signing up for too many tasks. But they did seem to find their groove, slipping into the roles for which they not only had a passion, but also a knack.

I soon was amazed at how this group of friends all fit together like an enormous puzzle with intricate pieces. Although they had a common purpose, they also had individual qualities that allowed them to find their niche. And they each had a reputation that drew those who needed help in the areas in which they were gifted.

If you were in search of someone you could count on to pray with and for you, you reached out to Pat. She was the best listener and prayed harder and more specifically than anyone I knew. She would ask for updates about what she was praying for. Hurting souls flocked to her.

Another gal was so creative when it came to teaching young children. She could make Bible stories jump off the page and into the hearts of the children listening to her. She found her place leading vacation Bible school in the summer and teaching a Sunday school class during the school year.

Still another older and elegant woman had a knack for fashion and makeup, which might not seem like a very spiritual quality to possess. But I tell you what, she was the most encouraging woman who helped draw others out of their shells. She made you feel beautiful, not only by helping you discover what style of clothes or color of makeup to wear, but by her encouraging words that made you feel confident no matter your size, shape, or color.

And finally, one of the women was skilled with decorating. If you needed to know how to rearrange your living-room furniture or what color paint to choose for your kitchen walls, she was the go-to gal. She helped you to maximize what you already had rather than having to go out and purchase a bunch of expensive new items.

All these women had the ministry of comfort. There are so many areas in life where we wonder if everything's going to be okay. It doesn't necessarily have to be a financial or physical area where we are perplexed and need reassurance. We might be worried about a relationship. We may fret over our future. We may stress about seemingly trivial things like our wardrobe or our homes.

When each of us uses whatever gifts we've been given to help meet a need or calm a nerve, we are giving comfort to others, sharing with them the reassurance we have already received from God.

Let's zero in today on your particular piece of the puzzle. Have you thought about what your purpose is in the body of Christ and in your circle of friends? Work your way through the following questions and make it a matter of prayer this week to discover what role God is asking you to play as you encourage others by sharing your gifts.

Back on day three of this forty-day challenge, we surveyed what passions or hobbies we had that could be used to serve others. We also explored what spiritual gifts we may possess. Today, let's drill down even deeper with a fun—but completely serious—exercise. We are going to write out a spiritual résumé.

A résumé is defined as "a brief written account of personal, educational, and professional qualifications and experience, as that prepared by an applicant for a job."[1] This job-finding tool typically includes your educational background, work experience, personal references, and even your hobbies. Once all this information is compiled, a potential employer has a snapshot of your skills and can place you in a role where you will fit nicely.

Well, there is no shortage of positions in the kingdom of God. There is always room for you to utilize your skills, gifts, and passions to serve others. Answer the following questions about your unique qualities in the categories provided. Then, feel free to turn to page 247 to transfer these answers to the designed spiritual résumé provided. You can do so by photocopying the résumé and filling in your answers by hand. Then, be sure to pray the prayer you sketch out at the bottom, asking God to help you find your purpose as he uses you to fulfill his purpose of bringing others to himself.

My Spiritual Résumé

Flip back to day three of this challenge, where you were asked to list three to five passions or hobbies that could be used to help or encourage others (on page 33). Choose your top three and jot them down again here.

1. _____

2. _____

3. _____

Next, what skills do you have that are not necessarily physical but are more relational? Are you a careful listener? Do you have a knack for helping others think through things logically when they are facing a decision, such as purchasing a new home? Maybe you are a cut-to-the-chase person who gives honest but helpful opinions in sticky situations.

Or perhaps you are just loads of fun and can cheer up others who are gloomy. List at least one relational skill below.

_____

_____

_____

_____

_____

Next, have you discovered what spiritual gifts you possess? (Remember, some resources for discovering them are listed on page 246.) List at least one—but up to three—of these gifts below.

1. _____

2. _____

3. _____

Lastly, write out a two- to three-sentence ministry prayer that takes into account your answers in the above sections. Here is an example:

> *Father, thank you for giving me a passion for crafting, as well as a love of lending a listening ear to those who are hurting. Help me to use these, along with my spiritual gifts of mercy and encouragement, to care for others, sharing the Gospel as I do.*

Now turn to page 247 to photocopy the spiritual résumé and transfer your answers onto it. Place the finished product where you will see it often, earnestly praying the prayer posted at the bottom asking God to help you play the part in this world he has already prepared for you.

Study AND Store

Memory Verse 4

Okay. Time for this week's optional memory verse. Post a copy of it from page 249 to aid in your memorization.

Praise be to the God and Father of our Lord Jesus Christ, the Father of *compassion* and the God of all comfort, who comforts us in all our troubles, so that we can comfort those in any trouble with the *comfort* we ourselves receive from God.

1 CORINTHIANS 1:3-4 NIV

day 18

Go Find Your Old Self

I sat on my twin-sized bed, curled up in my lavender bedspread, sobbing until I felt I had no tears left. My eleven-year-old self once again found her hopes dashed, causing a wave of grief that would only subside once exhaustion set in and sleep finally took over.

As a young child dealing with the fact that my father had wandered from the Lord, moving out of our home and leaving our family, never to return, that old bed became a familiar grieving ground. Later, as a teen, it held me when I was left out of my circle of friends, overlooked for the starring role in the play, or rejected by a crush I thought surely would notice me. Over the years, the four walls of my bedroom witnessed the heart-cries of a young girl trying desperately to navigate relationships and reality.

Then, at the age of sixteen, I met Jesus. My life took on a new beginning. But becoming a believer didn't change my circumstances. Not one bit. However, it *did* change my response to them.

I began to regularly spend time with my new mentor from the church—Miss Pat, the pastor's wife. She'd invite me into her home, pour me a cup of that apple cinnamon herbal tea, and offer me a homemade oatmeal cookie. As we got to know each other, I discovered that she had been through many of the same situations I found myself facing.

I listened as she gently encouraged me, teaching me where to take my sorrow, how to deal with my grief, and where to find comfort—in the security of God's relentless love. Her listening ear, loving advice, and prayers of consolation helped me through many rough patches of life. Today, more than three decades later, she is now in her seventies and remains a loving spiritual influence in my life.

This section's optional memory verse is a picture of this very concept: "Praise be to the God and Father of our Lord Jesus Christ, the Father of compassion and the God of all comfort, who comforts us in all our troubles, so that we can comfort those in any trouble with the comfort we ourselves receive from God" (2 Corinthians 1:3–4 NIV).

As Miss Pat thought about the ways God had comforted her in the past, she reached out to me with that same comfort, helping me deal with the various situations life brought my way.

When I relayed to her that I was facing discouragement as a child living in a broken home, with a now-absent father, she introduced me to one of the descriptions of God. He is a Father to the fatherless (Psalm 68:5). After a boyfriend dumped me for a rival on the cheerleading squad and I felt none of my friends really cared about the hurt in my heart, Miss Pat pointed me to the Father of compassion, the only One who completely understood my dilemmas and caused all my situations to work together for good, according to his purpose (Romans 8:28).

Today, as a mother of teenagers and young adults, I often find myself sitting with a new mom or a teen from a broken home. My mid-century dining-room table is a sacred space, drawing others in who long to have someone help process life's ups and downs. So, I bake my own oatmeal cookies and pour a steaming cup of coffee. I listen and I love. In many ways, I feel that in ministering to the people God sends my way, I am being like dear Miss Pat was to me. I am comforting others with the comfort I myself have received from Christ.

If we feel our life is lacking purpose, we have a very simple solution: Go find your old self and encourage her. Were you a lonely teenager? Reach out to one today, helping them process a relational challenge. Were you once a stressed-out mother, drowning in diapers and laundry? Find such a mom today and help to lighten her load. Kidnap both her kids and her dirty clothes. Give her some time to herself and then return her clothes, clean and folded, and her kids, happily fed. Did God allow you to survive an unwanted divorce? Reach out to someone in the same position today. Offer to take her out for lunch and provide an empathetic listening ear.

Go find your old self. Comfort her. Love her. Point her to Christ. When you do, you will find purpose in your past pain. And you'll be an example to someone who just might keep the circle of comfort going.

Ponder AND Pray

Have you ever thought of the idea of "finding your old self"? Ponder that concept now. When you think back on your life, what struggles have you had where God has met you? List two or three such situations below.

_____

_____

_____

_____

_____

_____

_____

_____

TAKE ROOT *and* TAKE ACTION

Key Scripture snippet: ". . . so that we can comfort those in any trouble with the comfort we ourselves receive from God."

How can you use the concept found in 2 Corinthians 1:4 to uplift someone in a similar situation today? Choose one of the scenarios above from your past. Now, is there someone in your current life who is facing a similar struggle? Write their name below.

_____

_____

Now, what specifically can you do to comfort them with the comfort that you yourself have received from God? Don't let your good intentions fizzle. Grab your phone and contact the person God has placed on your heart, or at least put it on your to-do list. Then, stand back and watch God use you as a means of comfort in the life of someone you know.

_____

_____

_____

_____

_____

_____

_____

day 19

Carving Out Time to Care

Look carefully then how you walk, not as unwise but as wise,
making the best use of the time, because the days are evil.

EPHESIANS 5:15-16 ESV

Whenever we are taking on a new endeavor, whether it is a responsibility at church or in our community, or just a personal goal like wanting to practice hospitality more often, the thought runs through our minds,

Where in the world am I going to find the time to do this?

Can you relate? Of course you can, my fellow strapped-for-time friend! Let's see if we can create a little white space in our calendars, making the best use of our time—as Ephesians 5:16 urges. That way, we can't use the excuse that we don't have enough time to live a life of hospitality. Here are a few strategies that can enable us to use our time resourcefully:

First, take inventory.

Get alone somewhere outside your house for an hour or so, taking along your calendar, a notebook, and a pen. A coffeehouse, park, or library works well for this outing. Scrutinize your schedule as it stands. Sketch out in the notebook what a typical week looks like for you right now.

Don't just include work commitments and appointments; jot down any responsibilities you have that pertain to your children, aging parents, or volunteer roles. Also include other ways you spend your time, such as exercising, housekeeping, grocery shopping, and even pastimes such as a hobby or watching television. Your goal is to have before your eyes, as accurately as you can, just how you are spending your time in your life right now.

Hold your too-full plate up to God.

Okay. Are you a bit frightened by what you see before you? Hold your too-full plate up to God, not clinging to anything on it. Prayerfully ask him what in your life needs to be scraped off to make time for caring for others. Don't buy the lie that if you back out of being involved in certain activities the world will not go on without you. They will be just fine. Don't give in to the curse of capability, taking on a task just because you feel capable, rather than called.

Delete.

Be honest now—and brave. What in your schedule needs to go? Resign from these responsibilities. I said resign, *not* re-sign up for tasks just because you always did in the past. Remove those activities God is nudging you to. Then ask the Lord to enable you to put back on your plate only those things he has called you to do.

Delegate.

All of us are going to have certain nonnegotiable aspects of our schedule we simply cannot suddenly step away from. But we can learn to ask ourselves this question about those chores and tasks: "Does it have to be me?"

For example, the housework. Does it all have to be done by you? Too many women take on all the responsibilities of the home, even though there are other human beings residing there. Could your husband start to perform a task you typically do in order to help ease your burden? And, if there are children in the house, even if they are only of elementary school age, they can help with some of the weekly and daily duties that need to be performed. Often, we have children who do too little, resulting in us becoming moms who do too much. Make it your goal to work yourself out of a job, enlisting the help of your kids with the tasks at home. My theory is that if a child can run a gaming controller or use a cell phone, they certainly can run a washing machine or dishwasher.

Divvy up the responsibilities among the people who live in your home and are old enough to perform them. Young children can become accustomed to setting and clearing the table, sorting laundry, and dusting or sweeping. Older children can help chop vegetables or brown meat. They all can learn to do laundry, wash windows, and scrub sinks and counters.

Know when—and when not—to multitask.

Look for pockets in your day where you could knock out two tasks at the same time. Can you fold laundry while also listening to a webinar that is required for work? Can you write some personal thank-you notes while sitting in the bleachers waiting for the basketball game to start? One favorite of mine was to clean the bathroom with nontoxic cleaning products while my children were in the bathtub. They were not infants or toddlers but were in early elementary school. They had fun splashing and playing with their Noah's Ark set. I didn't feel anxious, wanting them to hurry up. I simply cleaned the toothpaste out of the sink and wiped down the mirrors until they sparkled. I also folded washcloths and towels and put them away.

However, I highly caution against multitasking time when you should be paying attention to someone else. Don't be online paying your bills when your husband is trying to talk to you about something critical. Don't make out your grocery list when a teenager is trying to tell you about a horrid day he or she had at school. Know when—and when not—to multitask.

Shush the screens.

If you want to free up some time in your day, consider the amount of time you spend staring at a screen. It is estimated that the average person spends 144 minutes a day on social media.[1] That is 2.4 hours! That works out to be almost 17 hours a week! What?!? Yes, many of us spend as much time each week staring at a screen as would be needed to work a part-time job!

It's time we took control of our screens, rather than letting them take control of us.

Set limits on your phone in the settings section, if your cell phone has such a thing. Learn to mute or hide certain accounts that you really don't need to see. Set a timer each evening for fifteen or twenty minutes as you hop on social media to nose around for a while. When the timer rings, shut the social media scrolling down for the night.

Often, when many of us say we don't have the time for something, it really means we don't want to make the time because we are too busy doing mindless, trivial things like playing around on our phones. Oh, I'm not knocking it completely. It can be a wonderful tool. But we need to learn to ask ourselves if we are using it as a tool, a toy, or letting it morph into a major tangent that is knocking us off course when it comes to managing our time wisely.

Look for hidden opportunities right there in plain view.

Maybe you've taken all my advice and you still don't feel like you can free up a lot of time for having others over. Okay. But you can look for opportunities that are right before you, hidden in plain view. If your child is busy playing a sport and it is up to you to drive them there, sitting through all of the practices and games, make your role as a sports mom your mission field. Intentionally get to know some of the other parents. Show up with a treat to enjoy during the game. Buy everybody a round of hot cocoa or cappuccinos. You can seamlessly blend your desire for hospitality into some of the time commitments you simply cannot avoid.

Make it a matter of prayer.

Finally, make it a continued matter of prayer. Relentlessly ask God to help you clearly hear from him about just what you are to have on your schedule. Also ask him to create opportunities for you to get to know others and show them kindness, whether it happens within your home or when you're on the road. If God commands us to practice hospitality (Romans 12:13), he will make a way for us to obey that command.

day 20
Sensational Salads

*H*ere are a few fabulous salads to pair with a main dish to make a humble, but scrumptious meal to feed the people in your life. They are perfect to take to potlucks and community suppers as well.

Seven Layer Salad

This classic is from my husband's family. It just isn't an Ehman picnic without this on the menu—a unique blend of veggies in a delicious tangy dressing. Be sure to serve it in a clear bowl so the lovely layers show through. The amount of ingredients will depend on what size bowl you choose.

In a clear bowl or trifle dish, layer the following.

1. Iceberg lettuce, torn into bite-sized pieces
2. Chopped green peppers

3. Sliced water chestnuts, drained
4. Frozen peas, slightly thawed
5. Red onions, finely chopped

Then, spoon on the dressing (recipe below).

Finally, top with remaining layers:

6. Cooked, crumbled crisp bacon
7. Shredded sharp cheddar cheese

For the dressing: Mix the following ingredients. (You may need to double if making a large bowl.)

2 cups	real mayonnaise
3 tablespoons	white vinegar
3 tablespoons	sugar
¼ teaspoon	pepper
¼ teaspoon	salt

Thin with a little milk, if desired. Layer it up and dish it out.

Aloha Slaw

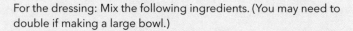

A fun and fruity island twist on a classic side dish. The almonds add a slight crunch.

Ingredients

4 cups	green cabbage, coarsely chopped
2 cups	cored, peeled fresh pineapple cut into ½-inch chunks
3	green onions, chopped

¾ cup	red bell pepper, finely chopped
2 tablespoons	white vinegar
1 cup	mayonnaise
3 tablespoons	white sugar
3 tablespoons	fresh lime juice
1 teaspoon	salt
⅓ teaspoon	ground black pepper
11-ounce can	mandarin oranges, drained
⅓ cup	sliced almonds

Directions

Mix cabbage, pineapple, green onions, and bell pepper together in a large bowl.

Whisk vinegar, mayonnaise, sugar, lime juice, salt, and pepper together in a separate bowl; drizzle over cabbage mixture and toss to coat. Gently fold in oranges.

Cover bowl with plastic wrap and refrigerate at least 2 hours before serving. Just before serving, sprinkle on sliced almonds. Serves 8.

Poppy Seed Pasta Salad

Not your garden-variety pasta salad. A little tangy. A tad bit sweet. If you want to make it a light main dish, simply add diced, cooked chicken, turkey, ham, or even drained canned tuna.

Ingredients

5 cups	(about one 16-ounce box) rotini pasta (gluten-free works fine)
2 16-ounce bottles	creamy poppy seed dressing
½ teaspoon	fresh garlic, minced

1 cup	cherry tomatoes, halved
1 cup	fresh broccoli florets, chopped small
½ cup	sliced black olives
2 cups	sharp cheddar cheese, cut in small cubes
½ cup	yellow bell pepper, chopped

Directions

In a large pot of salted boiling water, cook pasta until al dente; rinse under cold water and drain. Whisk together the poppy seed dressing and garlic.

In a salad bowl, combine the pasta, cherry tomatoes, broccoli, olives, cheese, and bell peppers. Pour dressing over salad, using 1½ to 2 bottles. Toss and refrigerate overnight. Serves 8–10.

Glazed Fruit Salad

This is as colorful as it is flavorsome. Great to take to a potluck or party.

Ingredients

20-ounce can	pineapple chunks in juice, drained and juice reserved
15-ounce can	sliced peaches in juice, drained and juice reserved
2 3-ounce boxes	vanilla cook-and-serve pudding (not instant)
4	bananas, perfectly ripe (not overripe)
15-ounce can	dark, sweet cherries in light syrup, drained
2 15-ounce cans	mandarin oranges in juice, drained
	Shredded coconut and/or chopped pecans for garnish

Directions

In a medium saucepan, whisk together 1½ cups reserved pineapple and peach juice and the pudding mixes. Bring to a rolling boil over medium-high heat, stirring constantly until thickened, about 5 minutes. Cool slightly.

In a large serving bowl, gently combine pineapple, peaches, bananas, and cherries. Fold in cooled pudding mixture. Gently stir in oranges. Store covered in the refrigerator for up to 2 days. Serve topped with shredded coconut and chopped pecans. Serves 8.

MEET THEIR *Needs*

day 21

Holy Land Hospitality

*A*s we flip our way through the pages of our Bibles—or tap our way, if we are using a digital form of Scripture—we encounter some well-known, as well as a few obscure, characters who serve as models for opening their hearts and homes. They shared the resources God had gifted them with, sprinkling thoughtfulness as they did.

Sarah, along with her husband, Abraham, encourages us to be willing to offer hospitality, even with short notice. In Genesis chapter 18, we read the account of Abraham, who was just minding his own business, hanging out near the entry to his tent. Suddenly three strangers appeared. He hopped up to greet them, lowering himself to the ground in a bow, as was the tradition in his culture at that time.

But Abe didn't stop with his stoop of welcome. He admonished them to stay, sharing the shade of his trees to help them cool off in the warm climate. He provided them with water to wash the dirt off their feet and even threw together a meal for them. The missus baked some bread while he roasted some meat on the grill and grabbed some milk to drink and cheese curds for the side dish of the day.

By blessing these strangers, Sarah and Abraham also got a blessing in return. It was through these three that God would build his plan for their family, letting them know a baby boy would soon be on his way. The drop-of-a-hat hospitality of this ancient couple encourages me at those times when I tend to stress about unexpected company appearing on my doorstep.

The strong and beautiful Abigail was also an exceptional case of someone showing hospitality, even in the midst of some not-so-lovely circumstances. In the book of 1 Samuel, chapter 25, we are given a look-see into her life. Although she was an astonishing woman, her husband, Nabal, was quite the jerk. He was rude, a liar, and had ghastly manners.

It was sheep-shearing time in the land, and Abigail's husband's flocks were out in the countryside grazing. The shepherd boy David, who would one day be king, was out with his boy band—I mean band of boys—in the wilderness of Paran. These dudes were a band on the run, fleeing from King Saul.

Out in the countryside, David and his crew had encountered Nabal's flocks and did not harm or steal them, as many wandering bands of blokes usually did. In fact, they'd been providing protection for Nabal's flocks. You'd think grumpy old Nabal would be grateful, but instead he called the group a band of outlaws, which royally ticked off the future king. David was soon on his way with four hundred men armed with swords to teach cranky Nabal a thing or two.

Abigail quickly sprang into action. She assembled a huge meal that included sheep, wine, bread, and even raisin and fig cakes for a sweet ending to the feast. Employing some donkeys as a DoorDash service, she sent the cuisine to David. She even apologized for her husband's atrocious behavior. David accepted her gifts and let her husband live. In true Old Testament reality-show manner, later Nabal was killed by God, and David ended up marrying the clever and resourceful Abigail.

In addition to dear Abby, a few New Testament women also led the way in hospitality. Lydia was a businesswoman we discover in Acts 16 whose first-century Etsy shop sold purple cloth in the city of Thyatira. She, along with her entire household, came to Christ after hearing the apostle Paul speak. When her heart was open to the things of God, she also threw open the doors of her home, allowing Paul and his companions to stay with her for a while.

Tabitha, also known as Dorcas, lived in the city of Joppa. Her reputation was renowned, we read in Acts chapter 9. She was known not only for her good deeds but also specifically for her love of the poor. She was quite the seamstress, often crafting beautiful garments. One day she tragically died. As her friends were preparing for the funeral, Peter appeared on the scene. As he took note of the deep love those of the village felt from her, it was through him that God performed a miracle. Tabitha was raised to life and got back to living a life of benevolence.

And perhaps my favorite models are the unnamed inhabitants of the island of Malta. In Acts chapter 28, these individuals welcomed a group of shipwrecked men that included the apostle Paul. Scripture actually goes so far as to say that they offered not just your ordinary welcome-wagon reception, but rather that they showed *extraordinary* kindness.

Why did they do this? Was it because Paul was a famous preacher? No. They didn't even know who he was. Was it because they shared the same political philosophy as the shipwrecked men? Nope. Read for yourself why they offered this unusual kindness:

> The local people showed us extraordinary kindness. They lit a fire and took us all in, *since it was raining and cold.*
>
> Acts 28:2, emphasis mine

They saw strangers with a need for warmth and then willingly—and without hesitation—gave it.

When we read of these instances of kindness and hospitality on the pages of Scripture, these people with their ordinary lives—mingled with the grace of God—give us a picture of love and welcome. Who in our lives is watching us, getting a glimpse of God's heavenly grace extended through our earthly hospitality?

Do they see us welcoming unexpected guests? Are we willing to make a meal, maybe even transporting it to someone who needs it? Will we eagerly throw open our doors and allow our homes to be used by those doing the important work of the church, perhaps allowing a life group or Bible study to meet there? Are we using our skills and talents to provide substantial good to others, so much so that one day, when we pass away, others will mourn the loss deeply? And, do we go beyond just being nice? Would others characterize our kindness as extraordinary and unusual? And—most important—do we offer it to others simply because they have a need, with no other ulterior motive?

Let's not stop at reading the example of these people of faith. Let's be a modern-day example of kindness and hospitality ourselves.

Below, compose a one-sentence prayer for the week, focusing on your desire to be someone who offers extraordinary kindness.

My
ONE-SENTENCE PRAYER
FOR THE WEEK

day 22

Enter Their World

*A*s part of her high school curriculum, my daughter was required to take a foreign language. She had tried her hand at Spanish in the seventh grade, but she wasn't a huge fan of that subject. When I suggested she take a Spanish course to fulfill her foreign-language requirement in high school, she said she had a different idea. She had done her research and discovered that American Sign Language also counted as a foreign language in our state. So she signed up to take a course at the local homeschool academy.

Not only did she find this course much easier than Spanish, but she also discovered that she could put it to real-world use. One day when she was accompanying me to the grocery store, she noticed that a man with a hearing impairment—a few registers over at the checkout line—was highly frustrated when attempting to communicate with the cashier about his purchase. She slipped out of our line and over to their lane and helped the man communicate with the cashier by serving as an interpreter. This gentleman was so grateful and gave her a huge hug of thanks. We saw his frustration and confusion melt away simply because somebody entered his world and spoke his language.

This is exactly what Miss Pat did when she invited me to play on the church softball team. She wasn't a huge athlete. I don't think she'd ever played softball in her life before. But she knew it was part of my world and so she made it a part of hers as well. I saw her do this on many occasions. She studied sign language when a family with a daughter who had a hearing impairment began attending the church. If she knew one of the teenagers had a particular hobby or interest, she brushed up on it. And this was long before the days of simply hopping on the Internet to do your research. She would haul herself down to the local library and check out a book to do her research.

My husband and I have discovered that entering the world of another person is imperative when it comes to parenting. We've learned about certain sports we never had interest in before. We've researched hobbies that our kids enjoyed. It sends a powerful message when we participate in something we don't particularly love in order to enter into the world of someone who does.

I think we see the same concept at work as we read the words of the apostle Paul, when he states that although he knows he is by law a free man, not enslaved by anyone, he chooses to behave in a way that enters another's world. He declares, "For though I am free from all, I have made myself a servant to all, that I might win more of them" (Corinthians 9:19 ESV).

The Greek word rendered "servant" here means a worker, held by constraint of law or necessity. However, it also is used in a metaphorical way. It can mean to give yourself wholly to someone's needs and service.

Now, there's a perspective we would all do well to live by when interacting with others. We should seek to give ourselves wholly to their needs and to be of service to them. It might not mean that we learn a whole new language so we can communicate with them, but how might we enter their world, being of service and meeting their needs?

Is there a young couple in your church whose child has just been diagnosed with autism? Hop online and research what type of environment is best for an autistic child. What might you do at your house in order to create such an environment?

Do you have a co-worker who is of a different nationality? Do your homework and figure out what type of cuisine is native to their homeland. Then, invite them and their family over for dinner one night and serve them that ethnic offering.

Making it your intention to enter their world not only speaks volumes of love to them, but it also broadens your horizons! I have tasted all sorts of delicacies from different countries, listened to music I would never have been exposed to, and learned about various sports and hobbies in which I had no interest. But I have to admit, it all was rather fun!

Start today to enter the worlds of others—and discover a whole new world yourself!

Let's focus today on learning to enter the world of another person in our life. God just may use this gesture to draw another soul into the kingdom. Spend a little time contemplating the following section. Record your responses in the spaces provided.

Ponder AND Pray

Think back over your own life. Was there ever a time when you felt somebody really made an effort to enter into your world? Who was it and what did they do that made you feel like they engaged with you in this fashion?

_____

_____

_____

_____

_____

Think about the various circles in which you interact currently. Prayerfully consider whether there is someone's name that rises to the top when you think of the concept of entering their world. Write that name below. After it, write at least one interest they have that you could learn about as well.

_____

_____

_____

_____

_____

Don't let your plan fall off your radar. Read a book. Do online research. Become well-acquainted with something they love to do and then make a date to do it with them. Below, sketch out a sentence or two stating what you might do to learn about their interest, and then use it to enter their world.

_____

_____

_____

_____

_____

Study AND Store

Memory Verse 5

For though I am *free* from all, I have made myself a *servant* to all, that I might win more of them.

1 CORINTHIANS 9:19 ESV

day 23

Share Your Stuff

*D*o you own the house you live in? Now, before you answer that, let me tell you that this is not some multiple-choice question where answers will vary from person to person depending on if they rent or own. All of us should answer this question the same way. With a resounding "No!" You do not own your home. Or your car. Or that fishing boat, if you have one. Your picnic table is not yours. Neither is your sofa or your favorite recliner. You don't even own your cell phone!

In reality, nothing you think you own actually belongs to you. It all belongs to God. Our earthly treasures and trinkets are only on loan for us while we walk the earth. If we keep this perspective in mind, it will totally revolutionize the way we see opening our homes and sharing our possessions with others.

I'd like to think that I set off in early adulthood with a heart bent toward hospitality. I was so excited to move into the first apartment when my husband and I married. It was the size of a postage stamp, but I didn't care. I couldn't wait to whip up something in the kitchen and whip open the door, inviting others in. However, as I accumulated more belongings, I started to get a little stingy with my stuff. Especially when we, along with most of our friends, started having children.

Oh, I still wanted to have others over for a cookout while we hung out, but when their kids broke my stuff, it made me steaming mad. Or when somebody wanted to borrow something, like my brand-new Crock-Pot— the one with all the bells and whistles that I had wanted for over two years—well, it was returned to me with a big chunk out of the crock and a dent in the pot. Now looking at my Crock-Pot made me want to cry.

Or the time we lent our car to someone and it was returned to us a little bit trashy inside, not at all looking like it does when my meticulous husband cares for it. (They call him the Q-tipper, if that gives you any indication of how he keeps things spotless. He cleans them with Q-tips!)

But one day, while lamenting to a friend of mine about yet another thing that got ruined at my house by the child of a friend, she offered a gentle rebuke. "Oh, Karen. Stop stressing. Those things don't belong to you anyway. When you use your stuff to minister to others, your stuff is gonna get broken."

I have come to see that she is completely right. But if my broken stuff can be used to reach broken people, it is all worth it. I just need to keep reminding myself that my things are not my own. Am I holding them with an open hand, or a closed fist?

Scripture addresses the sharing of our property with others. "If anyone has material possessions and sees a brother or sister in need but has no pity on them, how can the love of God be in that person?" (1 John 3:17 NIV).

When coming across that verse in the past, I always thought that meant somebody with a dire need, like they didn't have enough money for the groceries that month. I didn't think about it in the more subtle ways it might occur.

I might see a person who has need of a warm meal due to a recent death in their family. I might encounter someone who doesn't know how they're going to get to their medical appointment. In these instances, does it mean that if I have the means to make them a meal or give them a lift to their appointment but I don't, then how can God's love be in me?

Well, yes and no. In the original Greek, the phrase translated into our English as "has no pity" is a bit complicated to understand. Of course, it can be a lack of the empathy that leads to actions, such as making the meal or giving them the ride, but it goes even deeper than this. This phrase could also be translated as "closes the heart," as it is in several versions.

A deeper dive into the ancient language expands the meaning even further. It literally means to shut up the heart, and in this case the heart means your deep emotions, affections, and sympathy. Or perhaps the most vibrant rendering I found was "gut-level compassion."[1]

The original Greek word is related to one we have in English, *visceral*. It is an emotion that involves your physical body, not just your brain. It is sympathy and compassion that punches you in the gut or forms a knot in your stomach. Maybe it even sends a salty tear trickling down your face.

It doesn't mean that we can always physically meet someone else's need. That would be nearly impossible. We are not God, and we do have limited time and resources. But are we closing up our hearts, indifferent and apathetic toward their needs—or are we trying to be at least some part of the solution by passing on this need to someone who might meet it? And, at the very least, are we making it a matter of prayer?

Let's remember not only who owns our belongings, but whom we are serving with our very lives. Even though we may risk damaging our things, or putting a dent in our schedule, let's not close up our hearts toward the needs of others. Let's love and share like Jesus.

Time to focus on meeting the material essentials of others. Whom has God put in your world that you might help with even their most basic of needs?

Work through this next section to take inventory, then get ready to open your heart.

Can you recall any stories of a person or family who needed something considered essential for life, such as food, clothing, or shelter? Did others step up to meet this need? If so, describe the story below.

_____

_____

_____

_____

_____

It is so easy for us to take for granted the many blessings we have every day. Simple things like a warm bed to sleep in or a roof over our head that does not leak. If we don't have to worry where our next meal is coming from, we are fortunate indeed! When we live a life that has never lacked for these basic necessities, it's so easy to fail to appreciate them as we should.

Take a few moments to thank the Lord for the things you often gloss over because they have always been so readily available to you. Write down ten basic blessings you rarely stop and thank the Lord for.

1. _____

2. _____

3. _____

4. _____

5. _____

6. _____

7. _____

8. _____

9. _____

10. _____

TAKE ROOT *and* TAKE ACTION

Time to zero in on those in material need in your community. First, have you had any experience with being part of a group or project that met the needs of those less fortunate than you right there in your town? If so, what did you do?

_____

_____

_____

_____

Grab your computer, tablet, or phone and do a little research. See what agencies you can come up with in your community that have a mission to meet the physical needs of those who are hurting, poor, or in some other way less fortunate. Examples might include a shelter for battered women, a soup kitchen that serves the homeless, or an after-school program that provides snacks for children while also offering tutors to help with their homework. List any agencies or organizations you discover in the space below.

_____

_____

_____

_____

Next, write a sentence or two about what action you could take someday to be a part of providing for the needs of someone in your community. Could you spend a Saturday morning serving breakfast at a
shelter? Or maybe one Sunday afternoon you could help a local crisis
pregnancy center sort the baby clothing and diapers that are donated.
For added accountability, recruit the assistance of a friend who will go
with you to serve. Write both your intention and the name of any such
friend in the space here below.

Your Home, Their Airbnb

We have often had overnight guests come to visit for a night or two. Sometimes it was family members traveling through our state on vacation. Other times it was a batch of kids who crashed at our place for a slumber party. And on a handful of occasions, we actually have had someone live with us for an extended period of time.

Each of our kids, during their teen years, became friends with at least one person facing a tough time in their family relationally. Three or four of these young people stayed with us for a few days, or a few weeks, while seeking to strengthen or repair a relationship with a parent.

One day, our youngest son came home from school telling us of an eighteen-year-old senior he recently met who was soon to become homeless. He'd moved here from Tennessee to live with his grandmother and her husband and attend the local school for his final year. However, halfway through the year his grandmother's husband decided it cost too much money to have him living there. After all, six-and-a-half-foot-tall teen boys eat a lot. So his grandmother told him that even though she wanted him to stay, he needed to move out.

Returning to his home state would be unhealthy—perhaps even dangerous—so that was not an option. Our son begged us to allow him to move into our guest room. We said we were not at all comfortable having a complete stranger live with us. He then asked if we would just have this guy over for dinner once to see that he was a good kid. He knew that if we only would, we'd surely change our minds.

We changed our minds.

Having Jacob live with us for six months was a complete blessing. He called me Mama Karen. He ate dozens of boxes of Little Debbie Oatmeal Creme Pies and bottomless bowls of pulled pork. He was hard to wake up for school each morning and sometimes left his homework at home and I had to run it up to the school. He willingly went to church with us and loved eating meals together as part of our family.

He never once gave us an ounce of trouble.

This guy was just so thankful to have a safe place to live with people who actually wanted him there. When he graduated that June, I was a puddle. I didn't want him to leave. However, his dream was to join the military, so we threw him a graduation party, and off he went.

Now, God may not call you to have someone live with you for an extended time. However, there will undoubtedly be times when you will entertain guests overnight. Here are a few tips and strategies for making their time with you go smoothly.

Gather information. Before your guests arrive, quiz them about anything you might need to know to make their stay more enjoyable. Do they have food allergies or sensitivities? Do oil plug-ins give them a headache, so it would be best not to have one in the house when they are visiting? Be sure to inquire as to what might make their stay a comfortable one.

Do a trial run. If you don't have a regular guest room and instead your company will be sleeping on a pull-out couch or blow-up mattress, do a trial run. Try sleeping there yourself one night to make sure it is comfortable enough for your visitors.

Give them the grand tour. When they arrive, give them a quick but thorough tour of the house, pointing out anything they might need to know during their time at your place. Pay special attention to the kitchen so they feel comfortable helping themselves to a snack. Show them the best place to park their vehicle, making note of any ordinances in your city or township.

Clue them in to the quirks. While on the tour, be sure to alert them to any peculiarities in your home. Do you need to lift up on the doorknob on the front door in order to lock the dead bolt? Are the hot and cold faucets labeled backward in your century-old bathroom? Clue them in to any such quirks beforehand to ward off confusion during their stay.

Create space for their belongings. Your guest will have a suitcase with them, and perhaps some clothes to hang as well. Be sure to create ample space for their belongings and show them where to deposit them.

Give them a key to the city. Offer a quick rundown of places in your city they might be interested in visiting. A brochure or link to a website featuring such attractions would also be helpful. And don't forget to give them a spare house key to use in case you are not home.

Think technology. Provide your Wi-Fi name and the password on a note card on the nightstand near their bed. Also make sure they have a power strip to plug in their phone for recharging.

Recite your routine. Your guests will feel most comfortable if they know what to expect when it comes to your routine. Let them know what time you usually arise and have breakfast. Alert them to your work schedule and what time you will arrive home. If you turn in for the night early, let them know this as well.

Give them the proper send-off. Once your company has finished their stay, don't just send them off with a hug; also give them a small bag of snacks and a few bottles of water for the trip home.

Happy hosting!

day 25

Sips and Snacks

ry any of these scrumptious drink and snack ideas when you have company—overnight or otherwise. Delicious to consume as you visit with your guests.

Mocha Chip Frappuccino

You won't need to take a trip to the coffeehouse to enjoy this creamy—and chilly—concoction. Savor every sip.

Ingredients

10 ounces	very strong brewed coffee
8 ounces	whole milk
⅓ cup	sweetened condensed milk
1 teaspoon	almond extract
¼ cup	dark chocolate syrup
¼ cup	half-and-half

⅓ cup   semisweet chocolate chips
3 cups ice cubes
        Real whipped cream
        Additional dark chocolate syrup
        Mini semisweet chocolate chips, for garnish

Directions

Place coffee, whole milk, sweetened condensed milk, almond extract, chocolate syrup, half-and-half, and chocolate chips in a blender. Add ice and blend until smooth and icy, with tiny chocolate bits throughout. Serve in a glass with whipped cream, drizzled with additional chocolate syrup and sprinkled with mini chocolate chips. Serves four.

Almond Joy Hot Cocoa

Chocolate and almond dance together in this warm-'em-up mug of delightfulness.

Ingredients

1 cup   sugar
⅔ cup   baking cocoa powder
¼ teaspoon   salt
8 cups   whole milk
⅔ cup   water
1 teaspoon   vanilla extract
½ teaspoon   almond extract
½ teaspoon   coconut extract
1 7-ounce jar marshmallow creme

Directions

In a large saucepan, combine the sugar, cocoa, and salt. Stir in the milk and water. Stir over medium heat until thoroughly heated. Remove from the heat; stir in vanilla, almond, and coconut extracts. Serve in mugs topped with marshmallow creme. Serves six.

Cheesy Crab Bites

I adapted this from a recipe I found at a delightful retreat I spoke at a few years ago in West Texas. I do not care for crab, but I loved these.

Ingredients

1 5-ounce jar	Kraft Old English spread
6 tablespoons	butter, softened
2 teaspoons	mayonnaise
½ teaspoon	garlic powder
¼ teaspoon	Lawry's seasoning salt (or similar)
1 6-ounce can	chunk crab meat, drained
1 package	Bays English Muffins (I use only this brand. Thomas's brand is also good, but I wouldn't use off brands.)

Directions

Mix all ingredients but muffins, blending well. Spread mixture on muffin halves. Place on cookie sheet and freeze for 30 minutes. Cut into quarters. Store in freezer bags or bake immediately. To prepare, broil 6 to 8 inches from heat for 5–8 minutes until golden and bubbly. Makes 24 small pieces.

Heavenly Hash

This colorful snack always disappears fast. Serve with hearty corn chips for dipping. Yum!

Ingredients

2 cans	black beans, drained
3 cups	frozen corn, thawed and drained
1	red pepper, chopped fine
1	medium red onion, chopped fine
2½ cups	feta cheese crumbles
¾ cup	white vinegar
⅓ cup	olive oil
⅓ cup	white sugar
	Salt and pepper, to taste

Directions

In a medium-sized bowl, mix the beans, corn, pepper, onion, and feta cheese. In a small bowl, mix vinegar, oil, sugar, salt, and pepper. Pour over remaining ingredients. Store in fridge at least 2 hours. Drain slightly. Enjoy!

Homemade Cashew Caramel Corn

Super easy and amazingly delicious! Fun to make with your guests while you visit.

Ingredients

3 quarts	popped popcorn
3 cups	salted cashew halves
1 cup	brown sugar
½ cup	light corn syrup
½ cup	butter
½ teaspoon	salt
½ teaspoon	baking soda
1 teaspoon	vanilla extract
	Cooking spray

Directions

Preheat oven to 250 degrees. Spray a large shallow roasting pan, or cookie sheet with sides, with cooking spray. Spread popped popcorn and cashews in pan and place in oven to warm.

In a 2-quart saucepan, mix brown sugar, corn syrup, butter, and salt and bring to a steady boil over medium heat, stirring constantly. Boil exactly five minutes without stirring. Remove from heat. Immediately stir in baking soda and vanilla, mixing well.

Pour syrup over warm popcorn and cashews, stirring to coat evenly. Bake for 45 minutes, stirring occasionally. Remove from oven and spread on foil that has been sprayed with cooking spray. Cool and break apart. Store in tightly covered container. Makes about 15 cups.

Refresh
THEIR SOULS

Lose the Stipulations,
Keep the Love

The doctor's office I grew up going to offered all kinds of publications for children to read in the waiting room. I assume they were designed to take your mind off the stinging shot you were going to get from the nurse in the white dress who had a stiff cardboard hat sitting high on her head. Whatever the reason, I loved reading them.

One of the magazines had a section in it designed as sort of a brainteaser. On the top left corner of the page there was a picture drawn in great detail. Perhaps it was of a forest animal. Or maybe it was a scene of children playing on a beach. On the rest of the page were five other drawings that looked strikingly similar to the one in the top left corner. However, only one of them was an exact match. My elementary-school self spent those long minutes in the waiting room scrutinizing each drawing, attempting to discover just which one was a precise replica.

This isn't just something we do when surveying the pages of a magazine. Sometimes, we do this in real life. We fill up our circle of friends with only those people we deem are an exact match to us.

When our children were very small, I was a stay-at-home mom, and we homeschooled them. Although there are many arguments people make for homeschooling, some even feeling it is a biblical mandate, our main reason for educating our children in this manner was their father's work schedule. Had they enrolled in the public school, they would have rarely seen their father. Since he worked second shift at his factory, they would have said good night to him on Sunday night before going to bed and then not seen him again until he woke up around one p.m. the next Saturday afternoon. So, we decided to enroll them in the local homeschool academy two days a week, and then I taught them at home the remaining three weekdays.

At the time, we attended a church that was being planted and was made up of many of our close friends. At first we loved it, since so many of the families from the homeschooling community also attended. But soon we discovered that the lack of diversity actually was a downfall. Everyone lived a life almost exactly like us: stay-at-home moms, homeschooling their kids, with nearly the same income level and specific theological beliefs.

After about nine months, we clearly felt God calling us to attend a different church composed of people of various ages and stages in life, as well as those whose income level, race, or ethnicity was not the same as ours.

When it comes to opening our hearts and homes, we might easily be trapped into a mindset that includes only those who are nearly mirror images of ourselves. We might have unspoken stipulations that insist the people we invite into our lives and homes think, act, school, believe, and behave very much as we do.

Jesus actually warned against this in the Gospels.

> If you love those who love you, what credit is that to you? Even sinners love those who love them. If you do what is good to those who are good to you, what credit is that to you? Even sinners do that. And if you lend to those from whom you expect to receive, what credit is that to you? Even sinners lend to sinners to be repaid in full. But love your enemies, do what is good, and lend, expecting nothing in return. Then your reward will be great, and you will be children of the Most High. For he is gracious to the ungrateful and evil. Be merciful, just as your Father also is merciful.
>
> Luke 6:32–36

The Lord's words encourage us to stretch ourselves a little, not only showing love to those for whom it is easy for us to do so, but to reach out to those who are harder for us to love. To not shun the sinner. To not only rub shoulders with those who can repay the favor, but to love without stipulations, expecting nothing in return.

We might argue that we don't have any actual enemies in our lives. But let's learn to think of that term in a little different fashion. Don't think of the word *enemy*. Ask yourself who in your life are your *non-friends*.

Non-friends are those we gloss over. We don't hang out with them in real life or tend to view their accounts on social media. They are not numbered among our friends, either of the real-life sort or the cyber sort. Maybe this passage in Luke is encouraging us to expand our circle of friends to include some non-friends as well.

What does this look like when it comes to hospitality? It might translate into a series of questions we ask ourselves, such as: Do we only invite over the people we already know and like? Do we limit our invitations to people who have been good to us in the past, or do we step out on a limb and maybe invite over someone with whom we've had a little bit of a rough relationship? Do we invite another family over for a meal fully expecting that they will invite us over to their house in return? (I mean, after all, you've always been so curious what the inside of their house looks like, right?)

Heartfelt hospitality involves taking risks. We must be willing to go out on a limb to minister to whomever God calls us to love. Will it be at times someone from our close circle of friends? Of course! But there are also souls waiting to be refreshed with whom we don't already have a close—or even cordial—relationship. Will you dare to bust out of your secure and snug bubble and play your part in cheering and caring for others whether they be a friend, a casual acquaintance, or even someone with a prickly personality?

There is a holy satisfaction that comes to those who reach out and refresh the soul of another, without regard to who the person is. Let's love people . . . simply because they are people!

Below, pen a one-sentence prayer for the week on the topic of loving others without stipulations and despite their past or present choices.

My
ONE-SENTENCE PRAYER
FOR THE WEEK

day 27
Cravings of the Heart

Have you ever had a hankering for a certain snack, but you weren't exactly sure what you were craving? You just knew *something sounds good.* And so you began your quest.

First you flung open the cupboard and tried something salty, but the handful of barbecue potato chips really didn't hit the spot. So you reached into the cookie jar to devour an oatmeal chocolate chip cookie, thinking that might do the trick. But it didn't. And to the refrigerator you went. After rummaging around a minute, you found some leftover lasagna from last night's dinner. But even halfway through your warmed-up leftovers, you still didn't feel satisfied. You just weren't sure what it was you were really hungry for.

It's been my observation over the last three decades of growing in the area of hospitality that most people are craving something for their souls, although they're not sure what it is. Of course, at the very root of it all is their craving for God.

French mathematician and theologian Blaise Pascal asserted this innate longing when he wrote,

> What else does this craving, and this helplessness, proclaim but that there was once in man a true happiness, of which all that now remains is the empty print and trace? That he tries in vain to fill with everything around him, seeking in things that are not there the help he cannot find in those that are, though none can help, since this infinite abyss can be filled only with an infinite and immutable object; in other words by God himself.[1]

So, in order to help those longing for God to actually find him, what can we humans do? Can we help satisfy the cravings for Christ they have, even when they don't know what they are looking for? I think we can. We do this when we seek to meet needs they have emotionally and spiritually—needs they may have been trying to meet by other means, some of them not only unhelpful, but downright dangerous.

One thing I have seen often in people who have yet to meet Jesus is a craving for true acceptance, despite their past—or even present—choices. They want to be loved, flaws and all. Many teenagers who are not finding this kind of acceptance at home wander off and find it in a not-so-healthy place. That's not to say that all teenagers who may become intertwined with the wrong crowd feel unloved at home. Some, even if they have a fabulous home life, still make the choice to keep company with the corrupt. But the likelihood of this happening is higher if they do not feel loved and accepted for who they are by those to whom they are closest.

The dozen years my husband and I were involved in youth ministry, we saw this happen multiple times. Once our relationship with a teenager was at a place where we could candidly ask them why they chose the friends they did, often the answer was because they felt unconditional love in that particular crowd. If it was a crowd of ill repute, it could land them in hot water.

Is unconditional love something you personally seek to show others—especially to those who may be struggling or hanging out with the wrong crowd? Showing such love is like walking a fine line. We certainly do not want to condone any immoral, illegal, or unbiblical behavior. But we do want others to know they are loved despite their choices. At the same time, we long to see them come to faith in Christ that can severely alter their behavior. Basically, we want them to come as they are, just not to stay that way. We help pave the way for true heart change by God when we love without limits or conditions.

First Peter 4:8 (ESV) speaks to this endeavor:

> Above all, keep loving one another earnestly, since love covers a multitude of sins.

This verse tells us exactly how to love because it adds an adverb. In English the word chosen is *earnestly*. It also tells us to *keep* loving. Let's peek at the original meaning of these two qualifiers connected to the main verb *love*.

In the New Testament Greek, these two qualifiers were combined into one word. That word is *ektenés*. The meaning conveyed is *intentionally, constantly, intensely, and fervently*. The action illustrated is to love deeply and without stopping. Why? Because "love covers a multitude of sins."

Okay. Then just what does *that* mean? Isn't it a bad thing to cover up sin? I mean, aren't we supposed to encourage one another to confess our sins? (James 5:16). Again, we need to unearth the original meaning of the word *covers*.

This word, in its native tongue, means to *figuratively cover, conceal, or to envelop*. The thought conveyed is to hide from view. It does not mean to totally ignore or to look the other way. It doesn't mean we refuse to call a sin a sin. However, we also don't look at a person and only see their sin, failing to see them as an image-bearer of God, a person for whom Christ died.

In an extreme sense this would mean that if a person with a criminal record—who had committed a felony and had been incarcerated in the past—were to come to your home, you wouldn't mistakenly see their identity only with respect to their sin. You'd see them as a person, created in the image of God, who needs your love and acceptance. You wouldn't go so far as to wink at their sin, surmising that it was really no big deal. But you'd refuse to let their sin define them as you shirked away, afraid to engage kindly and lovingly.

Will you make it a matter of prayer to demonstrate love and show acceptance to someone who is craving to belong, yearning to be loved just as they are, without conditions or stipulations?

It is our job to love others and God's job to change them.

Ponder AND Pray

The first church I ever attended welcomed me with open arms, treating me as if I were the guest of honor, when in reality my heart was very far from Christ and my behavior was not in line with his Word. Has there been a time in the past when someone loved and accepted you despite your bad behavior? Briefly describe it below. (Note: I am not speaking of situations where someone who claims to be a believer is caught in blatant sin. This matter is discussed in 1 Corinthians 5:11 and is primarily a matter to be handled by the leaders in the church body to which they belong.)

_____

_____

_____

_____

_____

Look up the following verses and then jot down any principles you learn from them. It may be about how God treats us or about how we should treat someone who is not currently walking with the Lord.

Romans 2:11

_____

_____

_____

Romans 3:10

Romans 5:8

John 13:34

1 John 2:2

Ephesians 4:32

_____

_____

_____

1 John 4:8

_____

_____

_____

Study AND Store

Memory Verse 6

Okay. Time for this week's optional memory verse. Post a copy of it from page 251 to aid in your memorization.

> Above all, keep *loving* one another earnestly,
> since love *covers* a multitude of sins.
>
> 1 PETER 4:8 ESV

day 28

Fanning the Flames

eyond feeling unconditionally embraced by the first Christians who welcomed me into their church—and into their homes—there was something else that was an immense encouragement to me.

They believed in me and told me so.

It was at a very tumultuous and uncertain time in my life, when I was in the last few years of high school. I wasn't sure what my future held. I had some dreams about what type of career I wanted and the life I hoped to settle into someday. But when I thought of my future, it seemed like one huge, blinking neon question mark. Thankfully, I was graciously spurred on by members of the church who took the time to notice my good qualities—while overlooking my faults—and served as my cheerleaders.

I remember vividly a conversation with one woman. I was processing out loud with her various options for my future. There were a few colleges I was considering attending and likewise a few various majors. As she and I laid out the pros and cons, she listened patiently to my thoughts. What impressed me wasn't that she told me what she thought I should do. What impressed me was that she listened patiently and then said one simple phrase that has clung to my heart ever since.

She said she would pray with me about what the future held, because she had no idea which direction I would end up going. But regardless of what decision I made, she said she knew that I would be fine. Of course, this was primarily due to the fact that the Lord would be with me. But then, she tacked on an ending that warmed my heart and settled my soul: "Besides, I believe in you!"

She believed in me.

She believed in me long before I believed in myself. And her support both verbally and by her actions helped me to have confidence in myself and fanned the flames of the career and ministry I now have today.

Your words are powerful. They can be used to encourage another soul. So can your supportive actions toward a person and their current life situation. The word *encourage* means to impart courage, confidence, or hope to another person. What might that look like in your life today? Here are a few possible scenarios.

To the young mom raising babies and toddlers—wondering if she's even doing this mothering thing right—your help watching the kids so she can get things done around her home, coupled with a sincere "I believe in you," will boost her confidence and enable her to tackle the tireless and often thankless job of mothering with a renewed perspective and refreshed energy.

To the elderly neighbor—who is facing being a widow after losing her spouse of several decades—your family taking on the chore of raking her leaves, mowing the lawn, and shoveling the snow off her driveway will help to ease her troubled mind as she wonders how in the world she is ever going to function without her husband around anymore. After happily completing one of these tasks, with any family members who are available, deliver her a plate of homemade muffins, as you let her know, "You can do it. I believe in you. And our family is here to help with this tough transition."

To the college students who attend church with you but who hail from several states away, your home and your words can show them how much you care while helping to alleviate their loneliness as they navigate academic life. Invite them over to read and concentrate in a quiet room the week before their exams. But tell them to bring more than their books. Have them bring their laundry, and you can do it for them while they study. Or fix them a snack and bring them endless cups of coffee while they are cracking the books.

And while you are loving others with your actions, let them know you are praying for them and that you believe in them wholeheartedly. All of us reach junctures in our lives where we need to know that someone believes in us. Often this comes at a time of transition or when we are tackling a new endeavor.

By using your home, your resources, and your heartening words, you can help convey to someone that you believe in them while also sharing your faith as you do.

Ponder AND Pray

Who in your life right now is going through a transition or tackling a new venture? Write their name in the space below. Then, take a moment right now to pray for them, asking God how you might show them that you believe in them.

TAKE ROOT *and* TAKE ACTION

Brainstorming time! List two or three actions you could take that would help lighten their load or encourage the soul of the person you named above. Be specific and get creative. Ask yourself what you would like done for you—and said to you—if you were in their situation. You may not be able to follow through on all these ideas. Just list any possible actions you could take in the future.

1. _____

_____

_____

2. _____

_____

_____

3. _____

_____

_____

What are some encouraging words you could speak, whether in person, through a text message or email, or with a handwritten note? Write out a few sentences in the space provided below. Then be sure to tell them as well!

day 29

A Spa for Their Soul

he plane touched down in Charlotte, North Carolina, the town where my daughter lives. I turned my cell phone back on. Instantly it began to beep and buzz with various text messages that had been sent while I was in flight. One of them was from my daughter, who would be picking me up from the airport when she finished working at the hair salon she owns.

"Get ready for a treat!" the message announced. I assumed she meant that we would be going out to eat, since it was late afternoon and I hadn't had a meal yet that day. However, she had something else in store. She pulled her car up at the airport entrance, tossed my suitcase in her trunk, and declared that we were headed for the spa!

The spa? Wait . . . *what?* Although I was very familiar with the concept of such an establishment, I had never even stepped foot in one. I would soon discover that she was correct: I was in for a treat.

That day I was treated to my first facial, as well as a stress-reducing massage. It was divine! The room I lay in was dimly lit, with flickering candles adding to the tranquil atmosphere. Mist from an essential oil diffuser silently wafted through the air in the most soothing scent of lavender and lemongrass. In the background, the faint and delicate notes of classical music glided gently out of a speaker. I lay down, face-first, on a comfortable massage table, with my face sticking through an opening looking at the floor. Warm blankets enveloped me, making me nearly drift off to sleep. The massage therapist then used aromatherapy to further enhance my senses, swinging a pomander of rosemary and eucalyptus just below my face to soothe my sinuses.

After the ninety-minute hot stone massage was complete, I was in a state of physical and mental calm that I had never experienced before. Now if only my daughter's onetime splurge on me that day could be a weekly experience!

When we have a guest in our home, we can seek to provide a spa for their soul. A place where they can relax and unwind, and have their spirit refreshed. Then, when they leave our place, they can be better equipped to go back and tackle life after partaking in a mini retreat from the world. Just like a spa, let's focus on their five senses and on their physical and mental comfort. Here are some tips to try:

The sights. It's hard to relax in a room that looks like a clutter bomb blew up. So, as much as you can, seek to have the room in which you will entertain your guests clear of debris. It's great if it is also free of dust and has been vacuumed. However, I find in my experience it's more vital to not have junk lying around than to be sure it will pass a white-glove dust test. Your guests can probably put up with a tiny bit of dust better than they can deal with navigating toys strewn all about the floor, piles of soiled laundry dotting the furniture, or dirty dishes all about. Do a quick sweep of the room where they will be sitting and tidy it up as best you can.

The smells. Invest in a good oil diffuser, oil plug-in, or even some clean-burning candles made with essential oils and non-lead wicks. This will enable you to have your place smelling delightful whether you choose a sweet citrus, a warm spice such as clove or cinnamon, or something calming and soothing such as lavender, mint, or eucalyptus. Not only will the smell enhance their visit with you, it will also help to cement in their mind the time spent at your house. Of all our senses, our sense of smell is most closely tied to memories. Even today, when I smell something apple cinnamon, I am transported back in time to my mentor Pat's house. It brings back such treasured memories.

The sounds. Don't forget that your guests have ears and will be listening for the sounds at your home. Can you play some relaxing instrumental music that is of a variety they like? Are they a fan of smooth jazz? Do they like a particular worship band? If they are a college student who has stopped over to study for a while, perhaps putting on some classical instrumental melodies designed to help the brain focus would be appreciated. Or perhaps they simply need some peace and quiet, so no sound at all would be the preferred route to go.

The temperature. Be sure the temperature in your house is comfortable. If it is in the dead of winter, you don't want them freezing. If it is smack-dab in the middle of summer, you don't want them dripping with sweat either. Be sensitive to whether their body temperature happens to run hot or cold. No matter how warm I have it in our home for a particular guest, I still need to grab her a sweater when she is over because she always seems to be freezing.

The textures. Certain textures can also be very soothing to your guests. You may want to purchase a few fluffy pillows to toss on the couch as well as a luxuriously soft velour throw blanket for them to nestle in. And have you ever taken a nap using a silky, weighted blanket? Best. Sleep. Ever. You can often find these on sale, especially during a January white sale.

Their taste buds. Don't try to guess what foods your guests might like. Ask them! Discover whether they like sweet or salty. Are they a fan of crunchy snacks or partial to soft, warm comfort foods? Do they crave Asian cuisine, or would they prefer it to be taco Tuesday at your house, no matter what day of the week it is? Become a student of your guests, studying their likes and dislikes when it comes to all things edible. Then, be prepared with some of their favorites for them to munch on whenever they are at your home.

Their souls. Most of all, pay attention to their souls. Provide a listening ear without trying too hard to fix their problems, which can be misinterpreted as you trying to fix them! Share encouraging Scriptures or read them a portion of a book you think might be particularly helpful to their situation. And, if you feel comfortable and they do as well, offer to pray with them before they leave your home, specifically lifting up any concerns they may have to the Lord and believing together with them for answers.

Commit to using your home to provide a spa for your guests' souls. When you do, they will be in for a treat!

$day\ 30$

Pie, Oh My!

Grandma was right. There isn't anything a piece of homemade pie can't fix. Serve your guests a slice of one of these old-fashioned sweets and watch it lift their spirits. Note: Feel free to use whatever crust recipe is your standard one, but I have included my favorite at the end of this section. Also, if time is tight, the refrigerated, roll-out crusts work just fine too.

Triple-Berry Pie

This one snagged me the first-place blue ribbon rosette at the 1995 Michigan Clinton County Fair. Use fresh berries only, not frozen. Top with vanilla bean ice cream to really take it over the top.

Ingredients

2 homemade crusts, one for the top and one for the bottom (Note: My crust recipe is found on page 187.)

2 cups   raspberries
2 cups   blueberries
1 cup   blackberries
1 cup   sugar
1 teaspoon   almond extract
5 tablespoons   unbleached, all-purpose flour

Directions

Preheat oven to 350 degrees. Line pie pan with one crust. In a medium-sized bowl, gently mix raspberries, blueberries, blackberries, and sugar. Sprinkle on almond extract and flour, mixing carefully. Place filling in crust-lined pan. Roll out top crust and place on top of filling. Seal crust edges well and pinch to crimp. Prick crust all over with a fork and bake at 350 degrees for 55–60 minutes, just until bubbly and crust is lightly golden. Serves 8.

Sweet Potato Pie with Streusel Topping

"Song, song of the South. Sweet potato pie and I shut my mouth!"[1]
You won't want to shut your mouth when you make this creamy dessert. You'll want to open wide and devour a piece . . . or two!

Ingredients

1   homemade pie crust (Note: My crust recipe is found on page 187.)
¼ cup   all-purpose, unbleached flour
¼ cup   brown sugar
2 tablespoons   butter

¼ cup	chopped pecans
1½ cups	canned, drained, mashed sweet potatoes (or yams)
⅔ cup	sugar
½ cup	evaporated milk
3	large eggs
2 teaspoons	vanilla
½ teaspoon	nutmeg
¾ teaspoon	cinnamon
⅛ teaspoon	ginger
⅛ teaspoon	allspice (Note: may use 1½ teaspoons pumpkin pie spice in place of all the spices)
¼ teaspoon	salt
	Whipped cream and additional cinnamon or pumpkin pie spice for garnish

Directions

Preheat oven to 350 degrees. Line pie pan with pie crust and set aside. For streusel topping, in a small bowl stir together the flour and brown sugar. With a pastry blender, cut in butter until crumbly. Stir in pecans, mixing well. In a large bowl using an electric mixer, blend the sweet potatoes, sugar, milk, eggs, vanilla, nutmeg, cinnamon, ginger, allspice, and salt.

Pour into prepared crust. Top with streusel topping. Bake at 350 degrees for 45-50 minutes, until a butter knife inserted near the center comes out clean. Serve topped with whipped cream and sprinkled with additional cinnamon. Serves 8.

Apple Crumble Pie

Who doesn't love a slice of good old apple pie? Be sure to use a tart cooking apple. Eating apples such as Red Delicious will not work.

Ingredients

1	homemade pie crust (Note: My crust recipe is found on page 187.)
⅔ cup	sugar
¼ cup	all-purpose, unbleached flour
1 teaspoon	cinnamon
¼ teaspoon	allspice
¼ teaspoon	nutmeg
⅛ teaspoon	salt
6 cups	very thinly sliced, peeled cooking apples (Spy, Golden Delicious, Cortland, or Granny Smith)
¾ cup	all-purpose, unbleached flour
¾ cup	packed brown sugar, firmly packed
⅓ cup butter	cut in cubes

Directions

Preheat oven to 400 degrees. Line pie pan with crust and set aside. In a large bowl, mix sugar, ¼ cup flour, cinnamon, allspice, nutmeg, and salt. Toss in apples and mix well. Spoon into pie shell. In a medium-sized bowl, mix ¾ cup flour and brown sugar. Cut in butter until mixture is crumbly. Sprinkle over apples. Bake at 400 degrees on bottom rack of oven for 35–40 minutes until apples are tender. Serve warm with vanilla or caramel ice cream for the deluxe version. Serves 8.

Shoofly Pie

This recipe is from an elderly neighbor at my very first apartment in Three Rivers, Michigan. It is an Amish classic from the 1930s. It gets its name because it is so decadently sweet you'll have to shoo the flies away!

Ingredients

1	bottom pie crust (Note: My crust recipe is found on page 187.)
2	eggs
¾ cup	dark corn syrup
½ cup	sugar
½ cup	brown sugar
¾ cups	milk
½ cup (1 stick)	melted butter (no substitutes)
1 cup	quick oats
1 cup	sweetened, shredded coconut

Directions

Preheat oven to 350 degrees. Line pie pan with crust. In a large bowl, beat eggs with an electric mixer on medium speed. Blend in corn syrup, sugars, milk, and butter, mixing well. By hand, fold in oats and coconut and pour into unbaked pie shell. Bake at 350 degrees for 50 minutes or until set. Do not overbake. Serve with whipped cream. Serves 8.

No-Fail Pie Crust from Scratch

This makes enough for two crusts—a top and a bottom or two bottoms for single-crust pies.

Ingredients

5–7 tablespoons	ice-cold water
1	egg, beaten
3 cups	all-purpose, unbleached flour
¾ teaspoon	salt
1½ cups	shortening or lard, well-chilled
2 teaspoons	white vinegar

Directions

Place some ice cubes in a bowl to thaw, making ice-cold water. In a small bowl, beat egg with a whisk. In a large bowl, stir flour and salt together. Cut in shortening (or lard) and egg with a pastry blender, or two forks if you don't have one, until it resembles a coarse meal. Add 5 tablespoons of ice-cold water and the vinegar. Stir together gently until all of the ingredients are incorporated, adding more water if needed. It should form a firm but not overly stiff dough. Separate the dough in half. Form two evenly sized balls.

On a floured surface, roll out one ball of dough, starting at the center and working your way out. (Sprinkle some flour over top of the dough if it's a bit too sticky.) Roll out a circle about a half inch larger in diameter than your pie pan.

Center the rolling pin in the middle of the circle of crust. Gather each side up and fold over the rolling pin so you can transfer it to the pie pan. Gently press the dough against the corners of the pan. For a single-crust pie, go around the pie pan crimping the dough to make a clean edge. For a double-crust pie, leave edges hanging over the sides. Follow recipe for your specific pie.

Hospitality
OUTSIDE
THE HOME

day 31

The Proper Preposition

ave you ever heard the old saying that asserts, "Christians are to be *in* the world but not *of* the world"? What exactly is the difference?

Two distinctive prepositions are used in this charge—*in* and *of*. If you are *in* something, it refers to your setting—where you are physically located. If you are *of* something, it means you aren't just near in proximity, but you are an inherent part of it; your very being finds its source in it.

This old adage isn't just some glib platitude passed down from former generations of Christians. It finds its origins in Scripture, where Jesus himself addresses this concept in his prayer for his disciples and all who would follow him.

The content in John chapters 14 through 17 has been referred to as the farewell discourse of Jesus. In this intimate speech, Jesus conveys his final thoughts to his disciples just after they have shared the Last Supper in Jerusalem and the day before Jesus would be betrayed, arrested, and crucified.

At the close of John 17, we see the longest prayer recorded in all of Scripture. It is a prayer of passion, concern, and majesty and has been dubbed the High Priestly Prayer, since Jesus is our High Priest in the worldwide body of believers (Hebrews 2:17; 4:14–16; 5:6).

In this prayer—most likely spoken on the west bank of the Kidron Valley—Jesus lifted up his eyes to heaven, which was a customary posture of prayer for a Jew. His plea covered many areas of importance in the lives of his followers, including knowing God as the one true God, glorifying the Lord while on earth, and experiencing unity as Christians (John 17:3, 10–11).

Jesus then turns the words of his prayer to the tension that exists in dwelling physically here on earth while also refraining from adopting the mindset, habits, or beliefs of the world. He does not petition God to take his disciples out of the world, but to sanctify them in truth while they remain here on earth (John 17:15–17).

The Greek word translated to the English *sanctify* in John 17:17 means to set apart—to be different and consecrated. It also indicates to be pure, in stark contrast to things that are profane. It is important that we are daily allowing the truths of Scripture to sanctify us—set us apart—by altering our thoughts, words, and actions. We pursue this sanctification by the application of God's truth—his holy Word—to our daily lives.

Jesus didn't pray for God to isolate his followers, having them form their own exclusive club. He asked God to make them stand out in contrast to the world with regard to their behavior. Just as the brightly colored sprinkles on a birthday cupcake stand out *from*—and are not melted *into*—the buttercream frosting they are on top of, likewise believers are scattered into the world but are to remain distinct from it in behavior.

Jesus' petition wasn't only for the benefit of the eleven disciples who were with him that night. This prayer is for our benefit today as well.

God, through the Holy Spirit, can empower us to live in this world, rubbing shoulders with those who do not know him, while still being visibly different from them in our moral behavior. He will enable us to live in a way that displays the truth of the Gospel to those who are watching us. We do this not only by our actions but also through our verbal interactions with them, as we prayerfully and carefully look for opportunities to share the Gospel.

A few years ago, one of my sons played ball on a team made up both of boys from our church and of other players we didn't know. At the games, I chose to park my lawn chair in the midst of the moms I hadn't yet met. These women often entered into conversations that included language and topics you'd not usually find at your typical Bible study. However, I chose to take a genuine interest in their lives while also not entering into any of the questionable conversations that sometimes occurred.

When one of the most boisterous moms discovered I attended the church I did at the time, she exclaimed, "Are you kidding me?! I have lived in this town my whole life, and I've never had one person from that place give me the time of day. I thought they steered clear of me because I cuss and stuff and they think I'm going to hell. Why in the world are *you* so nice to me?"

God then opened a door for me to share what a delight it was having her for a new friend and how I believed Jesus would park his lawn chair in the middle of the rowdy crowd too, getting to know them. I praise God for prompting me to reach out. And I'm grateful he gives us the strength to get to know others who don't follow him without mimicking their behavior, allowing us opportunities to share his love as we do.

Do you hang out only in a holy huddle—rarely rubbing shoulders with people who are not believers? Or, would a quick look at your contact list show that you spend time with folks from all walks of life?

May the people in our lives observe our set-apart and sanctified ways not as us being better and more righteous in a holier-than-thou way. Instead, when they see us taking interest in them, may they desire to know more about the one true God we serve.

Below, write a one-sentence prayer for the week, asking God to enable you to live in the world without being of it.

My
ONE-SENTENCE PRAYER
FOR THE WEEK

day 32

Where Are the Layovers in Your Life?

*M*y husband and I stood at the cell phone store, waiting for our turn to upgrade our phones now that our latest contract was complete. Just then, a recent high school graduate our son was close friends with walked in the front door of the establishment. I hadn't seen him in almost a year, and instinctively my role as Mama Karen to any teenagers in sight kicked in.

"Dominguez!" I cheerfully exclaimed as I gave him a quick hug. (This guy preferred to go by merely his last name.) "It is *so* great to see you! Are ya hungry, honey?"

He got a puzzled look on his face. And then he sheepishly answered my pop question. "Umm . . . Mrs. Ehman. That's really nice of you. But . . . *we're in the Sprint store.*"

My husband and I both busted out laughing. For over three years, anytime this young man walked in our back door and into our kitchen,

I always asked him if he was hungry and then rustled up something for him to eat. Simply seeing him at the cell phone store made me kick back into mama mode, not even realizing we were out in public where I didn't have any food to offer him.

Here's the thing about hospitality—we can practice it no matter where we are. And the more we practice it, the more it spills over into all the places we frequent. While we typically think of being hospitable as applying to our own abode, it doesn't have to be limited to that. We can have a welcoming demeanor and an openhearted (and openhanded!) attitude no matter where we are. It just takes a little ingenuity and flexibility.

Let's start by asking ourselves this: Where are our layovers in life?

When traveling by plane, I often have to purchase a ticket that has at least one, if not two, layovers because I fly from a nearby small airport that doesn't have many direct flights. This means that I will spend a half hour or more in an airport in a different city, and usually a different state.

Sometimes these layovers can be several hours long. If the first leg of my flight gets delayed, I'm often thankful for these long layovers because they give me more time to catch my next flight. However, on the days that all goes smoothly, I can sometimes find myself grousing and complaining about being stuck in an airport without a lot to do.

Sure, I can take a book. Yes, there is usually Wi-Fi. But the time seems to pass so slowly on these traveling hiatuses. That is until I decide that they are assignments for me from God.

Instead of moping my way through the terminal, schlepping my suitcase behind me, I will find a café or coffee shop and order myself something hot and creamy to drink. But I also try to strike up a conversation with the barista who makes my coffee, finding out a little bit about them. Sometimes they barely grunt at me. Other times they spill their entire life story. And sometimes I have even discovered that they are a fellow believer and we've been able to encourage each other in the Lord.

On other stopovers I will go on a mission to brighten the day of somebody I bump into. Often, I try to apply the concept of finding my old self. So I typically will be on the lookout for a young mom wrestling with a couple of kiddos, trying to corral them and get them to behave in public. I will offer to help her unfold her stroller, or I will hold her diaper bag for her while she straps a child in. Often, I will slip her a little bit of money and tell her to buy herself, and her children, a treat. Seeing the smile light up her face makes what could've been a humdrum day of travel an adventure instead.

Of course, not all of us travel by airplane every week, but where are your layovers in life? At what places do you find yourself parked waiting during the week? Or what activities are your kids involved in that require your attendance as well? Does your place of employment have a break room where you find yourself a couple of times each day? Do you work out at a local gym or go to the same grocery store each week, often going through the checkout line of the same store employee? And what about places you hang out online on social media or various websites? You are certain to bump into people there as well.

"A generous person will prosper; whoever refreshes others will be refreshed," declares Proverbs 11:25 (NIV). There are many places each week where you will be in the world—whether in person or online. Let's determine this week to generously bring refreshment to those you meet along the way, making what could be a boring layover a blast instead!

Ponder AND *Pray*

Where are your layovers in life? In the space below, list any places you spend time each week. Then jot down any people you see on those layovers.

_____

_____

_____

_____

_____

_____

Now, in the space below, pen a prayer asking God to help you to go on an adventure, seeking to fill the layovers in your life with ministry as you listen to and encourage others.

_____

_____

_____

_____

_____

_____

_____

Memory Verse 7

A generous person will *prosper*; whoever
refreshes others will be *refreshed*.

PROVERBS 11:25 NIV

day 33

Serving Those
Who Serve You

hen my children received their yearbook one year from the homeschool academy they attended, there was a clever section that showcased all the workers at their school. The administrative assistant in the front office. The principal. The volunteer janitors. The lunchroom workers. This section was cleverly labeled *Necessary People*. These workers were important to the day-to-day functioning of this academic institution. Without them, life around there just wouldn't get done.

In each of our own lives we also have necessary people. They help us find the parsnips in the produce section of the farmers market. They groom our pets. They fill our prescriptions or touch up the gray roots of our hair. They make our highly particular sandwich at the local sub shop. Wherever we turn, we bump into another necessary person.

Yes, many of us remember such people when Christmastime rolls around. We may drop off a plate of cookies at the front office of our children's school. Or perhaps we set out a little sweet treat for the frazzled package delivery worker who is frantically making their rounds. But how many of us stop to remember such people on a random, ordinary day?

A friend of mine who was once an elementary school teacher told me that she could hardly remember the gifts she got at Christmas each year. However, what she never forgot was the handful of people who sent her a note, or gave her a little thank-you gift on an ordinary day, just to show their gratefulness for all she did in their child's life.

One aspect of the New Testament letters I love to take note of is the various ways the writer opens the letter, greeting its recipients in a personal and often unique way. One of my favorites is the opening of Paul's letter to the church at Philippi. He gives a very simple, yet somewhat profound, greeting:

> I thank my God every time I remember you.
>
> Philippians 1:3 NIV

Paul had developed a little habit. Every time one of his brothers or sisters from the Philippian church popped into his mind, it triggered gratefulness in his heart. So he thanked the Lord for them.

Can we adopt the same practice today? Whenever we remember, or encounter, a necessary person in our life, could we allow it to trigger a prayer of thankfulness to God, not only for that person, but for the various ways they help us to get life done? And then, could we take it a step further and actually let them know? What might this look like?

When we remember our faithful, dependable teenage babysitter, we could pick up a gift card to her favorite area restaurant and tuck it in a note card, along with our handwritten sentiments letting her know how grateful we are for her love and care of our children.

And while we do, we can whisper a prayer of thankfulness to God.

When we run into the clerk behind the department store counter who cheerfully rings up our purchases and never fails to inquire how our day is going, we can stop and verbally encourage them by telling them how much their cheerful attitude always makes our shopping trip pleasant.

And while we do, we can whisper a prayer of thankfulness to God.

When our mechanic is finished repairing the brakes on our car, making it safe again for travel, we can hand them a plate of homemade cookies and tell them how thankful we are for their hard work and expertise.

And while we do, we can whisper a prayer of thankfulness to God.

When we go to the school on an ordinary Tuesday afternoon to pick up a child, we can stop by the front office to drop off a gift card for a manicure at a local nail salon, thanking the administrative assistant for constantly using her hands to type away on the computer, keeping everyone in the district informed of what's going on at the school.

And while we do, we can whisper a prayer of thankfulness to God.

Being grateful is a healthy habit to cultivate. It helps us keep our eyes alert and our ears tuned to the various people around us whose hard work often goes unnoticed. And it increases our gratitude to God for the many blessings he sends our way through these often obscure but oh-so-necessary workers.

Ponder AND Pray

What necessary people in your life are you appreciative of? Make a list of at least five. Then, after each name, mention a few reasons why. Take a moment to pray for these individuals.

Name:

Name:

Name:

Name:

Name:

TAKE ROOT *and* TAKE ACTION

Take time in the next month or so to personally connect with at least one of these people, letting them know why you are thankful God placed them in your life. List the person below and what you will do for them.

day 34

Location, Location, Location

After living nearly a dozen years at our old home, we moved to a new town to be closer to my aging parents. We sold our home ourselves, something we have done four times now. And each time we looked for a new home, true to the real estate industry's catchphrase, the three things we took most into account when choosing a new place were "location, location, location!"

Well, today we are going to think about location, but not with regard to the place you call home. Today we are going to think of the many locations in which you find yourself every month, as well as the locations around your town where there are people just waiting for someone to notice them, appreciate them, and truly care. And finally, what are some long-distance ways you can love despite your location? So the entry for this day is less content and more workbook. Sound good? Here we go!

Read through the following questions and write out your answers. The goal is to discover what roles you currently find yourself in, the places those roles take you, as well as the various locations around your town—and across the world—where there are people waiting who would benefit from your kind and thoughtful actions.

First, let's start with your roles.

When I take inventory of the various roles I fill currently in my life, I can think of over a half dozen just when it comes to familial relationships. I am a daughter, sister, niece, wife, mother, aunt, and cousin. Name all the roles you have due to your family relationships.

When I think beyond my relatives, I can add the labels of friend, co-worker, neighbor, fellow life-group member, and church member. Think through your various commitments at church, in your children's schools, or in your local community. List as many as you can think of in the space provided here.

There are various locations to which I travel each month, meaning I can add more positions to the list. I am a customer at several businesses, a fellow gym member with many other folks down at the YMCA, a library user, coffeehouse frequenter, and repeat walker at the city park.

Think through a typical month in your life. To what locations do you travel in your community, whether you are a customer, a member of an establishment or organization, or just what appears to be a passerby? List these locations, specifically mentioning what part you play when it comes to them.

Lastly, I have relationships that are long-distance, whether they are people I know in person, or those I have met online. I am a blogger, an online friend, and a longtime friend of people I went to high school or college with or those I once lived near but who now live far from me. Contemplate your long-distance connections. List these in the space given, mentioning specific names if you can.

Time to spread some love! You won't be able to bless all the people covered above at once. However, this section will provide a go-to list for you to refer back to in the future as you scatter more kindness.

Today, prayerfully look over the lists you generated and choose just one person to bless. Then, try one of the ideas below. Put a star next to the one you will try first.

For those nearby:

- The next time you make a batch of cookies or muffins for your crew, double the batch. Deliver some to a neighbor.
- Take some veggies and dip, or a platter of fruit and nuts, to your church's office staff, or drop it off at an evening leadership meeting.
- Treat the fellow parents at one of your children's activities by showing up with a snack or beverages as you watch your kids play or perform.
- Gift a cashier, gas attendant, grocery bagger, bank teller, or other worker with a sweet or salty treat and a note attached thanking them for their diligent work.
- Buy a gift card to a local bakery and leave it on a co-worker's desk or taped to a friend's or neighbor's door along with a note telling them your life is sweeter for knowing them.
- Over-tip a restaurant server, barista, hairstylist, nail technician, or other such worker and attach a note thanking them for their faithful service all year long.

- Depending on the season, take a bottle of lemonade or iced tea, or a covered mug of hot cocoa or coffee to a local school crossing guard.
- At the holidays, drop off a plate of treats to a shut-in, elderly neighbor, or other person who may be lonely that time of year.
- Leave a wrapped treat in your mailbox for the mail carrier, along with a note of thanks. You can do the same for your package delivery person.

For those far away:

- Enact some "ministry of the mailbox." Resurrect the virtually forgotten art of handwriting on paper. Send a handwritten note of encouragement to a faraway friend or family member mentioning at least one thing you appreciate most about them.
- Share in secret, also as part of the ministry of the mailbox. Anonymously mail two five-dollar coffeehouse gift cards to someone, instructing them to use one and give the other away, paying it forward.
- Give the gift of prayer. Text someone far away who you know is going through a tough time, and pray for them.
- Tell five people on social media what you love most about them. Be sure to use lots of emojis or add an appropriate GIF. Write out a specific prayer you are praying for them.
- Hunt down a former teacher on Facebook. Leave a post on their wall with a specific memory you have of them. Thank them for pouring into your young life.

day 35

A Basket of Blessings

You can easily take your show on the road with any of these giftable goodies. Scour secondhand stores and garage sales for charming baskets to use to deliver your edible blessings.

Chocolate-Chip Pumpkin Bread

An autumn favorite I have gifted to my kids' teachers and coaches oodles of times. So moist, and the marrying of pumpkin to chocolate is an unbelievably scrumptious match.

Ingredients

4 cups	sugar
4 cups	pumpkin
2	large eggs, slightly beaten
1 cup	vegetable oil (I use cold-pressed virgin olive oil.)
5 cups	unbleached, all-purpose flour
1½ teaspoons	salt

1 teaspoon   ground cinnamon
1 teaspoon   ground cloves
4 teaspoons   baking soda
1 cup   chopped walnuts or pecans
1 cup   chocolate chips (or cinnamon or toffee chips)

Directions

Preheat oven to 350 degrees. In a medium bowl, beat together
sugar, pumpkin, eggs, and oil. Set aside. In a large bowl, stir together the flour, salt, cinnamon, cloves, and baking soda until well
blended. Using a mixer on medium speed, blend the pumpkin
mixture into the flour, just until incorporated. Gently fold in nuts and
chocolate chips by hand.

Pour batter into three medium-sized (8½ x 4½ x 2½-inch)
greased and floured loaf pans, spreading evenly. Bake 50–60 minutes at 350 degrees or until a cake tester inserted near the middle
comes out clean. Cool for 15–20 minutes and turn out onto a sheet
of aluminum foil. Let cool 15 more minutes, and then wrap tightly in
the foil. Keeps for 3–5 days on the counter or a week in the refrigerator. Yield: 3 medium loaves.

Walnut Crinkle Cookies

*This recipe has been passed down for years through my stepmom's
family. Her aunt won a blue ribbon with it at the Leelanau County Fair
in Traverse City, Michigan, back in the 1950s.*

Ingredients

2 sticks	real butter
2 cups	brown sugar
2	eggs
1 teaspoon	vanilla
2 cups	all-purpose, unbleached flour
1 teaspoon	salt
1 teaspoon	baking soda
3 cups	quick oats
1 cup	coarsely chopped walnuts (black walnuts are best)
1 or more cups	powdered sugar for rolling

Directions

In a large bowl, using an electric mixer, cream butter and sugar until fluffy. Beat in eggs and vanilla until well blended. In a medium bowl, stir flour, salt, soda, and oats. Beat flour mixture into butter mixture just until blended. Stir in nuts by hand until blended. Cover bowl and chill dough at least 4 hours or overnight. Preheat oven to 375 degrees. Shape chilled dough into 1½-inch balls and roll in powdered sugar. Place 2 inches apart on ungreased cookie sheet. Bake 10-12 minutes at 375 degrees. Do not overbake. Makes approximately 4 dozen cookies.

Sweet Cornbread Muffins

If you think cornbread can't be moist and delicious, you haven't tried this recipe. Place a dozen of these in a basket along with one of the homemade jams below, and you'll be sure to brighten someone's day—and delight their palate.

Ingredients

2	large eggs
2 tablespoons	clover honey
¾ cup	half-and-half
1¼ cups	unbleached, all-purpose flour
¾ cup	yellow cornmeal
⅓ cup	sugar
1 tablespoon	baking powder
¾ teaspoon	salt
½ cup (one stick)	butter, melted and slightly cooled, but not re-solidified

Directions

Preheat the oven to 350 degrees. Line a 12-count muffin tin with paper liners or spray with nonstick cooking spray. In a medium bowl, whisk eggs. Blend in the honey and half-and-half.

In a large bowl, stir the flour, cornmeal, sugar, baking powder, and salt. Pour the egg mixture over the dry ingredients and blend. Using a large rubber spatula, mix in the melted butter just until blended. Do not overmix! Carefully spoon batter evenly into prepared muffin tin, filling about ⅔ full. Bake for 15 to 17 minutes or until lightly golden. Cool slightly and remove from pan. Store covered at room temperature. May be frozen for up to 3 months. Makes 12 muffins.

No-Cook Strawberry-Banana Freezer Jam

This jam is delicious as part of a peanut butter sandwich. A certain husband I know has even been caught a time or two eating it straight out of the jar! (Hmm . . . I wonder who?)

Ingredients

2½ cups	prepared strawberries (approximately 8 cups fresh strawberries)
1 cup	prepared bananas (approximately 2 soft, ripe but not blackened bananas)
7 cups	sugar
1 pouch	liquid pectin (I use Certo brand.)
¼ cup	fresh lemon juice (You can use frozen, thawed 100 percent lemon juice, but do not use bottled ones that include chemicals.)
Five	pint (16-ounce) jars with rings and lids

Directions

In a large bowl, crush strawberries. Measure exactly 2½ cups prepared strawberries into another large bowl. Peel and mash bananas. Measure exactly 1 cup prepared bananas into bowl with strawberries. Slowly add sugar, stirring constantly to mix well. Let stand 10 minutes, stirring occasionally.

Stir liquid pectin and lemon juice together and add to fruit mixture. Stir until sugar is fully dissolved and no longer grainy, about 3–4 minutes.

Fill all jars immediately to within ½ inch of tops. With a clean, damp dishcloth, wipe off top edges of containers and cover with lids and rings. Let stand at room temperature 24 hours or until set. Refrigerate for up to a month or freeze for one year in a freezer.

Blueberry-Citrus Marmalade

I scored another blue ribbon for this jarred fruit spread. Gift it along with some English muffins and a few bags of fruity herbal tea.

Ingredients

1	medium-sized lemon
1	medium-sized orange
¾ cup	water
⅛ teaspoon	baking soda
4 cups	fresh blueberries, crushed
½ teaspoon	ground cloves
5 cups	sugar
6-ounce pouch	liquid pectin (I use Certo brand.)
7	half pint (1 cup) jars, lids, and bands

Directions

Using a very fine grater, zest the lemon and orange, letting the zested peels fall into a large stainless-steel Dutch oven or kettle. Add water and baking soda. Bring to a boil and then simmer, covered, for 10 minutes, stirring occasionally.

Squeeze the juice from the lemon and orange and add to the pan, being careful not to allow any seeds. Finely chop the remaining lemon and orange pulp and add it along with the crushed blueberries and cloves to the pan. Cover and simmer for 12 minutes.

Add sugar and bring to a full rolling boil over medium- high heat. Boil hard for 1 minute, stirring constantly. Remove from heat and immediately stir in the pouch of fruit pectin. Skim off the foam; stir and skim for five more minutes. Fill the jars with the hot marmalade. Cool slightly, and then, with a clean, damp dishcloth, wipe off top edges of containers and cover with lids and rings. Store at room temperature for 24 hours or until set. Refrigerate for up to a month or freeze for one year in a freezer.

WHOSE
Eyes
DO YOU HAVE?

day 36

Grab the Right Glasses

When I was a sophomore in college, I started having headaches. I also began having a hard time making out the words on the whiteboard in the front of the classroom, no matter how far down front I sat. So I made an appointment with an optometrist to check things out. The verdict? You guessed it. I needed glasses.

Once I began wearing them, my headaches and blurry vision swiftly disappeared. Recently, however, my eyes began to trouble me again, bringing back the pain in my brain. My optometrist suggested my migraines were coming from the quantity of time I spend looking at my laptop screen each day as an author. So she prescribed a new set of glasses to be worn only in front of the computer—made without my prescription for seeing long distances, but only with the magnification needed for seeing things that are just an arm's length away. This solved my dilemma, and I wear these mid-distance glasses in my home office and then don my regular glasses—or contacts—the rest of the time.

A few weeks ago, I backed out of the driveway to run a few errands. As I began to drive forward, I noticed that all the mailboxes and houses on my street were extremely blurry. I wondered if something was again awry with my vision. Then I realized I had forgotten to take off my computer glasses. I turned my vehicle around in the neighbor's driveway and headed back to my house to grab the proper pair.

You know, sometimes we look at our lives through the wrong lens and what we see can be a bit blurry—maybe even boring. However, if we begin to look at our lives through the lens God uses, we can view our seemingly ordinary lives in a clearer way, and our calling here on earth—however mundane it may seem—begins to come into focus.

I think we spend most of our time just reacting to what we see going on in the natural world. Our jobs, activities, community happenings—even our children's interests—usually set our schedules. And then it's off to the races. We frantically try to keep up with all the activities we see scrolling along on our calendar app each day. But all the while, we are oblivious to what is happening in the spiritual world and on the fringes of our days.

Behind the scenes, God is at work. He is the great dot-connector who can tether our hearts to the hearts of others. We can observe him change lives for eternity, if only we will slow down and adopt his perspective— noticing others in need.

I wish I could say I do this naturally. I don't. However, I have a son who does. Once, when he was ten years old, the kids and I took a trip to the oceanfront in North Carolina. On the way home, as we stopped at an intersection in Ohio, Spencer spotted a homeless man holding up a cardboard sign. He had just opened a Snickers bar and wanted to go give it to the gentleman, but I took off before he had time to tell me. He began to cry, begging me to go back. I was trying to keep to a schedule and wanted to keep going. However, his thoughtfulness tugged at my heart, so I changed my mind and turned around. However, when we returned to the corner, the man was gone.

Later, when Spencer was in middle school, I often noticed quite a bit of money being used some days from his lunch account—way more than was needed for a typical meal. He admitted he often bought food for classmates who had run out of money for the month. And as an adult, I've seen him pay for the groceries a woman ahead of him was about to put back because she didn't have enough cash on her.

Even if we don't come by it naturally, as Spence does, we can grow a heart for the marginalized, to help give voice to the downtrodden. We can notice those people who least expect to be seen. When we reach out to help, encourage, and love such people, we aren't just doing it for them. As Matthew 25:35–40 declares, we are doing it for the Lord himself.

> For I was hungry and you gave me something to eat; I was thirsty and you gave me something to drink; I was a stranger and you took me in; I was naked and you clothed me; I was sick and you took care of me; I was in prison and you visited me.
>
> Then the righteous will answer him, "Lord, when did we see you hungry and feed you, or thirsty and give you something to drink? When did we see you a stranger and take you in, or without clothes and clothe you? When did we see you sick, or in prison, and visit you?"
>
> And the King will answer them, "Truly I tell you, whatever you did for one of the least of these brothers and sisters of mine, you did for me."

As our forty-day challenge winds down to a close, let's purpose together to ask the Lord to give us the proper perspective as we view others through his eyes. May we not be blind to what is happening in the spiritual realm, but may we cooperate with God, loving earthly souls with a heavenly perspective.

In the space provided, create a one-sentence prayer for the week, centered on your desire to use your eyes and ears to notice those who least expect to be seen.

My ONE-SENTENCE PRAYER
FOR THE WEEK

day 37
Lifting Up the Beaten Down

My mother is not at all as outgoing as her talks-incessantly-to-anyone-who-will-listen daughter, but her quiet, loving actions spoke volumes to me while I was growing up. Mom was always on the lookout to help those less fortunate than her. She was a single parent living on a budget so tight it squeaked, but she gave generously of her time and money to people who felt beaten down in life.

She taught me that whenever I felt my life wasn't the greatest, I should remember there is always someone out there who is worse off than I am. Then, I should go find that person and do something to make their day. When I do, it will make my day as well! Mom was right, and living this way models what it means to offer love and aid to the people society often forgets.

In Jeremiah chapter 22, we see that God himself is genuinely concerned about doing justice, displaying righteousness, and caring for the plight of those who are oppressed.

> This is what the LORD says: Administer justice and righteousness. Rescue the victim of robbery from his oppressor. Don't exploit or brutalize the

resident alien, the fatherless, or the widow. Don't shed innocent blood in this place.

Jeremiah 22:3

It seems that for added emphasis, God's instructions begin with the phrase, "This is what the LORD says." This expression, used more than four hundred times in Scripture, indicates that the human being—in this case, the prophet Jeremiah—is not merely giving a suggestion conjured up in the mortal mind. The person speaking out loud is verbalizing the direct words and commands of the immortal Creator.

These behaviors Jeremiah relays to the people from the mouth and mind of the Lord may come across as overly familiar phrases to us today. Additionally, they are often easy to skip past since we may feel they don't apply to individuals but rather to government. To be certain we not only understand these directives but also apply them, let's look at their meanings in the original Hebrew and take note of to whom these instructions are given.

First, the meanings of the phrases from this verse:

Administer justice: Carry out the proper procedure with an honest and fair decision rendered.

Administer righteousness: Show appropriate vindication, specifically from the rulers of a government.

Rescue the robbed: Aid and defend those who have been forcefully taken from.

Don't exploit: Do not mistreat, oppress, or subdue.

Don't brutalize: Do not injure, either physically or ethically.

The resident alien: The sojourner, stranger, newcomer, or immi-
grant with no inherited rights.

The fatherless: The orphan who is helpless and thus susceptible to
injury.

The widow: The husbandless who is easily exposed to oppression
and harsh treatment.

Shed innocent blood: Kill a person even though they are not guilty
of any crime or moral failure.

Just reading the above list can incite various emotions. We may feel
overwhelmed with sadness for the vulnerable. We may be overcome with
anger at those who would take advantage of fellow image-bearers of God
(Genesis 1:26–27). At the very least, we may feel powerless to make any
real difference in such a huge social problem.

The plight of the oppressed, mistreated, and marginalized is both
chronic and colossal. But isn't it enough to just make sure *we* don't mistreat others in any of the ways mentioned in this passage? Perhaps these
directives were meant only for those in leadership in government.

Our answer is found when we back up to the prior verse, Jeremiah
22:2:

Hear the word of the LORD, king of Judah, you who sit on the throne of
David—you, your officers, and your people who enter these gates.

Seeking justice and righteousness is not left to the elite who are in
governmental power but also to the common citizens of a nation. It isn't
merely an optional hobby for a select group of believers. It is an imperative command that we see not only in today's reading but elsewhere in

Scripture as well, in places like Isaiah 1:17, Proverbs 31:9, and Psalm 82:2–4.

While we will most likely never see complete justice for those who are oppressed in our lifetime, we can do our best to play a part in alleviating the suffering of those with whom we can connect (Hebrews 13:16; Deuteronomy 15:11). We can reach out to those without family (Psalm 68:6). We can work to help the foreigners who reside among us, treating them with compassion (Leviticus 19:33–34). We can care for widows and orphans (James 1:27).

Most of all, we can pray and look forward to the time when Jesus himself rights every wrong, the One who boldly declared that he came to proclaim good news to the poor and liberty to the captives, to deliver recovery of sight to the blind, and to set at liberty those who are oppressed (Isaiah 61:1; Luke 4:16–21). When we reach out to those whom society rejects or forgets, we don't do it to be noticed; we do it because we are serving the Lord himself when we do.

Ponder AND Pray

We've talked a lot about the individual communities in which we reside. Now let's reach out beyond our own towns. Are there any organizations you are aware of that help alleviate the suffering of any of the groups of people mentioned in today's entry? Write their name in the space below. If you are not familiar with any, go on a little Internet search to see if you can discover such an organization or ministry.

Record the name of this organization in your prayer notebook, if you have one. Or write it on a sticky note or type it in as the screensaver on your phone. Commit to praying for them over the next week and contributing financially, if you have the means to do so.

Study AND *Store*

Memory Verse 8

And the *King* will answer them, "Truly I tell you, *whatever* you did for one of the least of these brothers and sisters of mine, you did for *me*."

MATTHEW 25:40

day 38

Who'd You Bring with Ya?

On the weekends, my front foyer is hardly ever clean and cleared. Instead, it houses up to a dozen pairs of shoes that have been deposited there by their owners who are either invited or impromptu guests in our home.

Years ago, it was the teenagers from the youth group at our church or perhaps a few of the squad members from the cheerleading team I coached at our local high school. As our family grew, the pile of shoes belonged to the moms and children in our play group or the adults from our life group at church. Once my kids got into middle school and high school, an assortment of baseball and football cleats, volleyball shoes, dance slippers, and other diverse footwear lay heaped in a pile.

Most recently, the mountain of shoes belongs to my youngest son's friends. Usually they have come over to play cards or watch a sporting event in the family room in our basement. Often, I am in my home office working, and I don't even realize that my son is back home or that anyone arrived with him. However, I will then notice the shoe stack as I saunter past it on my way from my office to the kitchen to grab another cup of coffee.

228

About that time, my son will bound up the stairs to grab some more snacks for his gang of guys. A little surprised to see him, I often say the same thing to him when he gives me a quick hug and a kiss on the cheek. "Oh, hey. You're home! Who'd you bring with ya?"

Then he will rattle off a list of names. These dozen or so boys have become "sorta sons" to my husband and me. I love them like family. Even if they make my grocery budget skyrocket. It's been a pleasure over the years getting to know them and helping them process life as they sit at our table, enjoying a bowl of cheesy corn chowder or finishing off the last piece of the peanut butter apple crisp in the pan.

I'd like to say that it's always a pleasure to have these guys over, but I would be lying. There are times their presence sort of cramps my style, especially when I'm under a book deadline. I don't like to be interrupted. And I like a quiet house when I am attempting to knock out a lot of pages on the project at hand.

Usually I'm pretty safe if I get up really early on a Saturday morning to work on my manuscript. I can work in peace with the guys soundly sleeping downstairs. That is, until Second Grant moved to the school district and became part of the posse. (There already was a Grant in this group, so I called the new guy Second Grant.)

Second Grant is an early riser. He would often plop himself on the couch next to me early on a Saturday morning and ask, "Hey, Mrs. E. What ya working on?" It broke my concentration, but I would try to sweetly answer him. Before long, he made himself a cup of coconut mocha coffee and sat back down on the couch. Finally taking the hint from God that the soul sitting next to me was more important than the words on my screen, I would shut my laptop and try to get to know him.

I endeavored to naturally weave the topic of Jesus into our conversations. Usually I was pretty subtle, but some of the other boys knew they were typically going to get a free sermon from Mama Karen, served up alongside their homemade whole-grain oat waffles with whipped butter and pure maple syrup.

I purposed to practice with Second Grant what I call "in the moment ministry." Martyred missionary Jim Elliot said, "Wherever you are, *be all there*. Live to the hilt every situation you believe to be the will of God."[1] Deciding to "be all there" is practicing "in the moment ministry," zeroing in on the person before you without fretting about all of the other things you could be doing. It includes giving them eye contact, leaning in to really listen, being fully present with both your body language and your brain.

After about nine months of my spending some "in the moment" Saturday mornings hanging out with Second Grant, he asked me if my husband and I were going to be around on the second weekend of March. Assuming there was some big sporting event happening that the boys wanted to watch at our house, I asked him what the big game was and what kind of snacks they wanted. It was then that he gave a reply that made my jaw drop and my spirits soar.

"Oh, there's no game on. I wanted to let you know that I have accepted Christ and I'm getting baptized that Sunday. I want you and Mr. Ehman to be there if you can."

I instantly felt incomparable joy but also a twinge of guilt as I thought back to how many times I felt like his desire to talk with me was an interruption of the important work I was trying to do. But it wasn't an interruption. It was the actual important work. And you can bet that my husband and I were there in the congregation that night as not only

Second Grant, but also his brother and his mom, were baptized into the faith. Just thinking of that night still makes my heart smile.

You know, when we get to heaven someday, I like to imagine what the Lord will say to us. I don't think we are going to be congratulated on our successes in our careers. We probably won't be applauded for our parenting or congratulated on any other earthly endeavors we undertook and were successful at. Do you know what I imagine the Lord saying to us? The same thing I say to my son when I notice that he and the shoe pile have arrived at our place.

"Oh, hey. You're home! Who'd you bring with ya?"

Who'd you bring with ya?

Ponder AND Pray

What do you think of the concept of "in the moment ministry"? What keeps you from behaving this way?

Using the space below, craft a prayer to God asking him to help you have his eyes to see the people you may feel are interrupting your day as the important work he has for you.

_____

_____

_____

_____

_____

_____

TAKE ROOT *and* TAKE ACTION

Think of one person you feel God might be calling you to practice "in the moment ministry" with. Write that person's name in the space provided below. What can you do in the next week or two to show them you care? Jot this down after their name and add it to your calendar.

_____

_____

_____

_____

day 39

Filling Up So You Can Keep Pouring Out

a story in Luke 10 tells of two sisters and how they spent their time when Jesus came one day for a visit. Martha was busy scurrying to get to the end of her "to do before company comes" list, but Mary chose a different route. She settled herself at Jesus' feet, soaking in his words and his presence.

Living with a heart given to hospitality can be draining—not only physically, but emotionally, mentally, and even spiritually. Perhaps today we can set aside our own to-do-before-company-comes lists until we've mimicked Mary, spending time with Jesus, filling up so we can keep pouring out. Let's stop scurrying and be seated instead. There is always plenty of room at his feet.

Here are a few practical ways to slow down and soak in the presence of Jesus. Intentionally and habitually spending time with him will enable us to pour into others without feeling completely drained.

First, hand your to-do list over to Jesus.

Sometimes it is so hard to hear the Lord's voice through all of the hustle of our day. We stress and obsess about our to-do list and our many appointments. The best way to focus in on our time with God (and to leave our to-do list behind) is to take our to-do list along with us!

Get alone and get quiet. Ask God to bring to your mind all that you must get done. Make a list of these things. Then, spend time praying through each item on the list.

As God brings more tasks to your mind, write them down. Don't worry that it is unspiritual to stop halfway through a prayer and jot an item down. It helps you to clear your mind and then allows you to focus better on your time alone with God. He is concerned about all the details of our life, even if it is our plan to go grocery shopping or run to the drugstore.

Next, get deliberate.

Treat your time alone with God as seriously as any other appointment you have. When you have to go to the dentist, you brush your teeth and make sure you show up on time. Why do we assume our time alone with God will just happen spontaneously? Learn to treat it with intentionality. Enter the time you will spend with God in your digital calendar or write it in your paper planner. You can even set an alarm on your phone. Have a designated time and stick to it.

Read and write.

Get ahold of a journal to use alongside of your Bible. Don't just read the Bible. Write your thoughts down too.

Keeping a journal will help you grow your relationship with God. You will process as you write out your thoughts. Also learn to both read and write prayers. Read prayers in the book of Psalms out loud to God. Then, write out your own specific prayers to him. It will amaze you when you go back later and see the ways God answered your prayers.

Record yourself reading Scripture and use it to help you memorize.

Have you ever vowed to memorize Scripture but then failed to follow through? One way to remedy this is to memorize verses by listening to them over and over again in your own voice. Use your phone's voice memo app to record yourself reading out loud any verses or passages you would like to commit to memory. Then, pop in your headphones and listen to the verses each day as you walk, do housework, or cook dinner. It makes it so much easier to cement the words in your mind this way!

Give your brain seventeen minutes a day off.

A few years back, I was listening to a podcast. I sure wish I remember who the speaker was, but I don't. What I do remember, though, was the assertion she made. The woman speaking was an expert on how our brains function, especially when it comes to the tension between productivity and rest. She made a challenge to the listeners. It is one that I took to heart, and I've tried to do ever since, although I'm not always 100 percent successful. Her theory? Everyone needs to attempt to spend seventeen minutes a day doing and thinking absolutely nothing. Oh my! This is a Herculean feat for me.

I have always been jealous at my husband's ability to shut his brain off and simply think nothing. When he's staring off into space as we sit on the picnic table in our backyard, I ask him what he's thinking about. He will claim, "Oh. Nothing."

HOW DO YOU DO THAT!?!

Since listening to the podcast, I have made it my aim to sit in a chair, looking out the window, and just let my brain rest. I find for me it works better in the middle of the afternoon, because my brain is so ready to jump into work first thing in the morning. However, I can honestly say that this mini respite helps to calm my heart rate, clear my mind, and even focus more successfully when I do get back to work. So, decide that you too will give your brain a seventeen-minute break each day.

You know, even Jesus spent time away from the crowds. And he beckoned his disciples to do the same:

> He said to them, "Come away by yourselves to a remote place and rest for a while." For many people were coming and going, and they did not even have time to eat.
>
> Mark 6:31

If we heed Jesus' advice to go away with him to a quiet place, we can strengthen our spirits and refresh our souls, positioning us for further—and more effective—ministry in the future.

Private moments spent with Jesus—soaking in both his Word and his presence—will prepare us to open both our hearts and our homes for his glory, touching lives for eternity as we do.

day 40
Calendar-Year Cakes

*H*ospitality is a year-round practice. To assist you in this endeavor, try your hand at some of these seasonal and holiday cake recipes. May they help you make endearing memories for decades to come.

Fruit of the Forest Mocha Cake

Chocolate and berries or cherries combine for this decadent dessert perfect for any special occasion. It is even more marvelous when served slightly warm and topped with natural vanilla bean ice cream.

Ingredients

1¾ cups	unbleached, all-purpose flour
½ cup	cocoa powder
1½ teaspoons	baking soda
1 teaspoon	salt
1 cup	sugar
½ cup	brown sugar, packed
½ cup	butter, room temperature

½ cup	buttermilk
¼ cup	brewed coffee
1 teaspoon	vanilla
3	eggs, divided
21-ounce can	blackberry, raspberry, blueberry, or cherry pie filling (I buy the variety that is free of artificial colors and flavors.)
1 cup	sugar
2½ tablespoons	cocoa powder
½ cup	unbleached, all-purpose flour
½ teaspoon	salt
1 cup	boiling water
3 tablespoons	real butter
1 teaspoon	vanilla

Directions

Preheat the oven to 350 degrees. In a medium bowl, stir together the flour, cocoa powder, baking soda, and salt. In a large bowl, using an electric mixer on medium-high speed, cream the sugars with the butter until fluffy. Then, over medium speed, add buttermilk, coffee, and vanilla, blending well. Beat in the egg yolks until well combined. Mix the dry ingredients into the butter ingredients, until just combined. Mix in the pie filling until well-blended. Lightly beat egg whites with a whisk for 1 minute until frothy. Mix the egg whites into the batter at low speed, blending completely.

Spray a 9 x 13-inch pan with cooking spray and lightly dust with flour. (You may also use a cooking spray made for baking that already has flour in it.)

Spread the cake mixture into the pan and bake for 40 minutes at 350 degrees or until a cake tester comes out clean. In a medium saucepan, mix 1 cup sugar, 2½ tablespoons cocoa powder, ½ cup flour, and ½ teaspoon salt. Pour 1 cup boiling water over the dry mixture along with 3 tablespoons butter. Cook slowly over medium heat, stirring with a wire whisk constantly to prevent lumps from forming, until thickened but still pourable. Remove from heat and whisk in 1 teaspoon vanilla. Immediately pour over hot cake, spread evenly, and allow to cool. Cover with foil and store in the refrigerator. Serves 12.

Cranberry-Orange Pound Cake

The amalgamation of tart cranberries, sweet orange, and crunchy nuts makes this moist, heavy dessert unforgettable!

Ingredients

1½ cups (three sticks)	salted real butter, softened
2¾ cups	sugar
6	large eggs, room temperature
1 teaspoon	vanilla extract
2½ teaspoons	grated orange zest
3 cups	unbleached, all-purpose flour
1 teaspoon	baking powder
¼ teaspoon	ground nutmeg
½ teaspoon	ground cinnamon
½ teaspoon	salt
1 cup	sour cream
1½ cups	chopped fresh or frozen cranberries
⅓ cup	chopped pecans or walnuts

Vanilla glaze:

1 cup	sugar
1 tablespoon	unbleached, all-purpose flour
½ cup	half-and-half cream
½ cup (one stick)	butter
½ teaspoon	vanilla extract

Directions

Preheat oven to 350 degrees. In a large bowl, cream butter and sugar until light and fluffy. Add eggs, vanilla, and orange zest, beating well. In a medium bowl, stir together flour, baking powder, nutmeg, cinnamon, and salt. Add flour mixture to creamed mixture alternately with sour cream. Fold in cranberries and nuts.

Pour into a greased and floured 12-inch Bundt pan. Bake at 350 degrees for 65–70 minutes or until a cake tester inserted in the center comes out clean. Cool for 15 minutes. Remove from pan to a cake plate to cool completely.

In a small saucepan, combine sugar and flour. Stir in cream and butter. Using a whisk, bring to a boil over medium heat, stirring constantly. Boil for exactly two minutes. Remove from the heat and stir in vanilla. While still warm, pour over cake. Serves 10–12.

Banana Cake
with Peanut Butter–Cream Cheese Frosting

This was the first cake my daughter helped me make for her dad's birthday when she was three. The flavor trifecta of banana, peanut butter, and cream cheese is a home run!

Ingredients

2 cups	sugar
¾ cups	salted real butter, softened
3	large eggs
1 teaspoon	real vanilla
1½ cups	buttermilk
1½ cups	really ripe bananas, mashed (about 2–3)
1 teaspoon	lemon juice
3 cups	unbleached, all-purpose flour
1½ teaspoons	baking soda
¼ teaspoon	salt

Frosting:

2 teaspoons	real vanilla
¼ cup	salted real butter, softened
½ cup	creamy peanut butter
1 (8 ounce) package	cream cheese, softened
3½ cups or more	powdered sugar

Directions

Preheat oven to 350 degrees. In a large bowl, combine sugar and butter, and cream until fluffy. Mix in eggs, one at a time, and vanilla. Stir in buttermilk, bananas, and lemon juice. In a medium bowl, combine flour, baking soda, and salt, stirring well. Add dry ingredients to wet ingredients and beat at low speed just until well blended. Bake in two 8-inch round cake pans that have been greased and floured.

Bake at 350 degrees for 22–28 minutes or until a toothpick comes out clean. DO NOT OVERBAKE. Cool 15 minutes and remove from pans.

In a medium bowl, blend all frosting ingredients with a mixer on medium speed until well blended. Place the first cake on a cake pedestal and top with frosting. Place second cake on top and frost the top and all sides. Cover and store at room temperature. Serves 12.

Vintage Chocolate–Mayonnaise Cake

My mom makes the best birthday cakes. Besides baking one for our birthdays, she made one for us each year on the first day of school. This rich, chocolate confection from the 1950s was in her repertoire. And yes—mayonnaise is the secret ingredient! So moist and decadent.

Ingredients

1 cup	water
1 cup	mayonnaise (Do NOT use low-fat, fat-free, or salad dressing.)
1 teaspoon	vanilla extract
1¼ cups	sugar
2 cups	all-purpose flour
4 tablespoons	baking cocoa
2¼ teaspoons	baking soda

For chocolate buttercream frosting:

⅓ cup	softened butter
⅓ cup	cocoa powder, sifted
1¾ cups	powdered sugar
¾ teaspoon	vanilla
1 to 2 tablespoons	milk

Directions

Preheat oven to 350 degrees. In a large bowl, use an electric mixer on low speed to mix the water, mayonnaise, and vanilla until well blended. In a medium bowl, combine the sugar, flour, cocoa, and baking soda. Mix the dry ingredients into the mayonnaise mixture just until blended. Do not over-mix.

Pour batter into a well-greased and generously floured 9-inch square baking pan. Bake at 350 degrees for 30 minutes or until a toothpick inserted in the center comes out clean. Remove from oven. Cool 15–20 minutes and invert onto a cake pan.

To make frosting, using an electric mixer in a medium bowl, beat butter until light and fluffy. In a small bowl, stir cocoa and powdered sugar together. Add half of the cocoa mixture to the butter and blend well. Beat in vanilla, blending completely. Add remaining cocoa mixture and beat until smooth, adding milk as needed. Finally, frost top and sides of cake. Serves 6–8.

Your Final (and Continual) Assignment

$\mathcal{I}$ am just about ready to shut my laptop and hit the "send" button on the manuscript for this book. Once I do, I need to clean our house that I have been sorely neglecting as I wrote. The fridge is nearly empty. There are bills to pay. Laundry to fold. And I need to order more refills for my favorite erasable pens. My mind is mulling over all these tasks as I get back to everyday life.

Just a minute ago, I heard the familiar ping on my phone notifying me that I have a new email. I took a break to click my way over to see it. The message was from my friend Young, who is the director of the Michigan State University campus venue of my home church, Riverview. He asked if I would provide some food for two college events coming up—a monthly Wednesday worship time as well as an overnight weekend lock-in.

These might seem like insignificant assignments. After all, college students will eat nearly anything. I could just send some store-bought cookies and a bag of chips. But making food for a brood of ravenous students is a holy task that I am honored to do. It is a way to humbly serve the Savior.

In the midst of my usual routine, I can grab my mid-century aqua mixing bowl and whip up some lovin' from my oven, praying that my tasty treat will play a part—however small—in making someone feel welcomed, wanted, and lavishly loved by the God of the universe.

Do not spurn the small assignments God drops in your lap. Perform them with as much vigor as you would if they were highly visible and important tasks.

Wrap them in love.

Bathe them in prayer.

And smile when another weary heart is soothed, a convert is made, or you simply sense God using ordinary you to assist him in his high and holy work of drawing all people to himself.

> This is good, and it pleases God our Savior, who wants everyone to be saved and to come to the knowledge of the truth.
>
> 1 Timothy 2:3–4

May you spend the rest of your days opening your heart and sharing your home with the souls God guides your way.

I am praying for you.

Karen

Acknowledgments

To my agent, Meredith Brock, for your tireless efforts, creative ideas, and willingness to talk while you are out running carpool and I'm home folding laundry.

To editor Jennifer Dukes Lee, for a simple email, an important invitation, and for cheering me on as I wrote this book.

To my Proverbs 31 Ministries family, especially President Lysa TerKeurst and Executive Director of Communications Glynnis Whitwer. I love serving God with all of you.

To my prayer team made up of ninety-three fabulous women, for hitting your knees on my behalf. I couldn't—and wouldn't want to—do this without you.

To my spectacular assistants, Kim Stewart and Dana Herndon, for your stellar skills and constant support.

To my mother, Margaret Patterson, and my spiritual mother, Pat Beasley, for teaching me how to follow Jesus.

To my family, husband Todd and children Kenna, Jason, Mitchell, Macey, and Spencer—three of whom are biological and two who are by marriage, but I forget which ones are which. I love us. Yes, loud, bickering, beautiful us.

To Jesus, for taking my place on the cross and offering me a forever home in heaven. Indescribable.

Resources

Spiritual Gifts

On day three, we talked about spiritual gifts and using them to serve others. If you have never studied this topic—or discovered what gifts you possess—check out the resources below intended to help you in this venture.

Websites

I want to make clear that the best way to discover your spiritual gifts is to survey those Christians closest to you. However, online resources can also be helpful in this journey. My favorite place for this is at LifeWay.com. They have online resources that include both a list of the gifts—along with where they are found in Scripture—and an inventory for you to take to discover your gifts. Check it out at: https://www.lifeway.com/en/articles/women-leadership-spiritual-gifts-growth-service.

Books

The following volumes will help you learn about and unearth your spiritual gifts:

Spiritual Gifts: What They Are and Why They Matter by Thomas R. Schreiner; B & H Books; 2018

You Are Gifted: Your Spiritual Gifts and the Kingdom of God by Ken Hemphill; B & H Books; 2009

Understanding Spiritual Gifts (40-Minute Bible Studies) by Kay Arthur, David Lawson, and BJ Lawson; Waterbrook; 2010

Discovering Your Spiritual Gifts by Kenneth Kinghorn; Zondervan Publishers; 1984

Spiritual Résumé

My Top Passions and Hobbies

_____

_____

My Relational Skills

_____

_____

My Spiritual Gifts

_____

_____

My Personal Ministry Prayer

_____

_____

Be *hospitable* to one
another without complaining.
Just as each one has received
a *gift*, use it to serve others,
as good stewards of the
varied grace of *God*.

1 PETER 4:9-10

REACH OUT, GATHER IN
Karen Ehman

But if anyone does not
provide for his own *family*,
especially for his own
household, he has denied
the *faith* and is worse
than an unbeliever.

1 TIMOTHY 5:8

REACH OUT, GATHER IN
Karen Ehman

For the whole law is fulfilled
in one statement: *Love*
your *neighbor* as yourself.

GALATIANS 5:14

REACH OUT, GATHER IN
Karen Ehman

Praise be to the God
and Father of our Lord
Jesus Christ, the Father of
compassion and the God
of all comfort, who comforts
us in all our troubles, so that
we can *comfort* those in any
trouble with the comfort we
ourselves receive from God.

1 CORINTHIANS 1:3-4 NIV

REACH OUT, GATHER IN
Karen Ehman

For though I am *free* from all, I have made myself a *servant* to all, that I might win more of them.

1 CORINTHIANS 9:19 ESV

REACH OUT, GATHER IN
Karen Ehman

Above all, keep *loving* one another earnestly, since love *covers* a multitude of sins.

1 PETER 4:8 ESV

REACH OUT, GATHER IN
Karen Ehman

A generous person will *prosper*; whoever refreshes others will be *refreshed*.

PROVERBS 11:25 NIV

REACH OUT, GATHER IN
Karen Ehman

And the *King* will answer them, "Truly I tell you, *whatever* you did for one of the least of these brothers and sisters of mine, you did for *me*."

MATTHEW 25:40

REACH OUT, GATHER IN
Karen Ehman

Notes

Day 1: Holy Leftovers and Apple Cinnamon Tea

1. "5590. Psuché," Strong's Concordance and HELPS Word-studies, *BibleHub.com*, https://biblehub.com/greek/5590.htm.

Day 3: Open Your Gift (and Then Give It Away!)

1. "manifold," *CollinsDictionary.com*, HarperCollins, 2020, https://www.collinsdictionary.com/us/dictionary/english/manifold.

Day 16: Our Need to Nurture

1. Raj Raghunathan, PhD, "The Need to Love," *Psychology Today*, January 8, 2014, https://www.psychologytoday.com/us/blog/sapient-nature/201401/the-need-love.

Day 17: On Puzzle Pieces and Purpose

1. "résumé," *Dictionary.com*, 2020, https://www.dictionary.com/browse/resume-.

Day 19: Carving Out Time to Care

1. "Average Time Spent Daily on Social Media (Latest 2020 Data)," *Broadband Search.net*, https://www.broadbandsearch.net/blog/average-daily-time-on-social-media.

Day 23: Share Your Stuff

1. "4698. Splagchnon," HELPS Word-studies, *BibleHub.com*, https://biblehub.com/greek/4698.htm.

Day 27: Cravings of the Heart

1. As quoted in Thomas V. Morris, *Making Sense of It All* (Grand Rapids, MI: Eerdmans, 1992), 134.

Day 30: Pie, Oh My!

1. Bob McDill, "Song of the South," from Alabama, *Southern Star* (RCA, 1988).

Day 38: Who'd You Bring with Ya?

1. As quoted in Elisabeth Elliot, *Through Gates of Splendor* (Wheaton, IL: Tyndale House, 1981), 20.

KAREN EHMAN is a *New York Times* bestselling author, a Proverbs 31 Ministries speaker, and a writer for *Encouragement for Today,* an online devotional that reaches more than four million users daily. She has written fifteen books and Bible studies and is a contributing writer at the First 5 Bible study app. Karen has been featured on numerous media outlets including *TODAY* Show Parents, FoxNews.com, Redbook.com, Cross walk.com, and *HomeLife* magazine. Her passion is to help women live their priorities as they reflect the Gospel to a watching world. Married to her college sweetheart, Todd, the mother of three and mother-in-law of two, she enjoys collecting vintage kitchenware, cheering for the Detroit Tigers, and feeding the many people who gather around her mid-century dining-room table for a taste of Mama Karen's cooking. Connect with her at karenehman.com.

Know the Truth. Live the Truth.
It changes everything.

If you were inspired by *Reach Out, Gather In* by Karen Ehman and desire to deepen your own personal relationship with Jesus Christ, Proverbs 31 Ministries has just what you are looking for.

Proverbs 31 Ministries exists to be a trusted friend who will take you by the hand and walk by your side, leading you one step closer to the heart of God through:

- Free online daily devotions
- First 5 Bible study app
- Online Bible studies
- Podcast
- COMPEL Writer Training
- She Speaks Conference
- Books and resources

Our desire is to help you to know the Truth and live the Truth. Because when you do, it changes everything.

For more information about Proverbs 31 Ministries,
visit www.Proverbs31.org.

Proverbs 31
MINISTRIES